# Power, Greed, and Stupidity
## in the Mental Health Racket

# Power, Greed, and Stupidity in the Mental Health Racket

by Walter Fisher
and Joseph Mehr
and Philip Truckenbrod

**W**

THE WESTMINSTER PRESS
Philadelphia

PUBLISHED BY THE WESTMINSTER PRESS®
PHILADELPHIA, PENNSYLVANIA

PRINTED IN THE UNITED STATES OF AMERICA

**Library of Congress Cataloging in Publication Data**

Fisher, Walter, 1924–
  Power, greed, and stupidity in the mental health racket.

  Bibliography: p.
  1. Mentally ill—Care and treatment.  I. Mehr, Joseph, 1941–   joint
author.  II. Truckenbrod, Philip, 1942–   joint author.  III. Title.
[DNLM: 1. Mental disorders—Popular works.  2. Mental health services
—Popular works.  WM 30   F537p 1973]
RC439.F53          362.2          72–11599
ISBN 0–664–20958–0

To Irene, Nancy,
and Joan

# Contents

# Preface

It is clear that there are a large number of strange, deviant, and "crazy" people in our society. We do not have to look any farther than newspaper reports of assassinations and assassination attempts on men in public life to be reminded of this fact. We do not feel that it is unfair to say that the individuals charged with the societal responsibility of dealing with deviancy and atypical behavior have not made significant inroads in reducing cultural deviancy.

We believe that the primary stumbling block in attempting to deal with the problem of deviancy has been the society's emphasis on the medical model. We feel that it is a critical error in thinking to assume that all strange and atypical behavior is an expression of an inner "disease process." Although it seems possible, if not probable, that certain behavioral deviancy is an expression of an inner illness, we are suggesting that most behavioral disorders are expressions of a society's institutions and systems.

In this book we are attempting to provide new orientations, new attitudes, and new solutions to those behavioral problems which professional caregivers have been calling "mental illness" for the last two hundred years. There are a number of critical issues that have to be reconsidered. They are:

1. The responsibility of the deviant person

2. Our expectancies in regard to those persons labeled "mentally ill"
3. The nature of risk-taking and security
4. The possibility of mental illness
5. Classification systems
6. The professions—training and education
7. Community mental health
8. The human service model versus the medical model
9. The problem of sexuality in the mental hospital
10. Treatment technologies
11. Treatment through institutional change
12. The concept of "critical mass"

We should say that there are other caregivers like ourselves who are attempting to reconsider the traditional concepts in the field of mental health. In fact, although there are still many hang-ups, the Department of Mental Health in Illinois has gone through a virtual revolution in the last twenty years. Several of the directors have been extremely clever innovators and risk takers. In the material that follows, we hope to provide a new perspective on these issues for the attentive publics of the mental health system.

There are two informational items that we would like to bring to the reader's attention. The first item is our style of presenting references. If we quote from an author or cite an idea from an author, we present his name and the date of publication; for example, Reik (1964). If the reader wishes to read the reference, he can turn to the References at the end of the book and obtain the remainder of the reference information.

The second informational item concerns the use of the pronouns "we" and "I." Through most of the book the pronoun "we" is used, but in certain instances the material is so immediate and so personal that the senior author, Walter Fisher, feels the need to present the material in essentially an autobiographical fashion and thus turns to the "I" style of presentation.

At this point we would like to acknowledge our personal debt

of gratitude to our typists Mrs. Dorothy Lund and Mrs. Imo-
jean Deibert, who spent long hours of personal time working
on our manuscript. In addition, we would like to express
our intellectual debt to Norris Hansell, Harold Visotsky,
O. H. Mowrer, and Thomas Szasz. A special note of thanks
must go to Robert Agranoff for his insightful criticisms of the
manuscript content and his fruitful advice in regard to its publication, and to Daniel Manelli, superintendent of Elgin State
Hospital, for his continued interest and support of "treatment
through institutional change."

WALTER FISHER
JOSEPH MEHR
PHILIP TRUCKENBROD

*Elgin State Hospital*
*Elgin, Illinois*

# I

# The Mental Health Game Plan

Mental health, particularly as it is practiced in hospitals, clinics, and on the couch, is a constantly beleaguered and alienated institution. Legislators, muckrakers, and newspapers are continuously involved in the process of investigating and exposing the mental health consortium. As this process is going on, it is not difficult to imagine the public sitting on the sidelines, enjoying the various assaults and exposés, and adding a few of their own bitter "slings and arrows."

Mental health caregivers have typically responded to these critiques by requesting more funds, pleading for more employees, and, in true public relations fashion, promising an eventual "cure" or "vaccine" that will wipe out those dreaded "mental diseases." During the past two decades these critiques and subsequent caregiver responses have increased mental health budgets tenfold. However, this cycle of critiques, defenses, and increased funding has not met societal expectations. Moreover, mental health jargon has become a source of gross humor. An enormous credibility gap has developed as a result of the mental health experts' failure to meet their promises. Every investigation seems to demonstrate administrative incompetence, negligence of patients, and newly formed "snake pits" replacing old "snake pits."

Despite the biting attacks and gross humor at their expense, caregivers have continued to do business in their same old styles. It is amazing, to say the least, that for most of the twentieth century there have been few attempts to evaluate the efforts of the mental health professionals. The field has been packaged in a romanticism, mysticism, and jargon that supposedly resisted mundane observation and evaluation.

The reader can obtain some feeling for this mysticism in the following clinical quotation by Reik (1964): "A patient told me how on the previous day he had a violent quarrel with his girl [he had been having a sexual affair with her for a considerable time]. At first the conversation turned upon the girl's health; she had been feeling weak and poorly of late. She had remarked that she was afraid of tuberculosis; she weighed too little and must put on flesh. The young man, my patient, did not think that necessary. He opposed it on aesthetic grounds. . . . The analyst suddenly perceived . . . that the quarrel centered unconsciously upon the question of a child. Looking back, I discern that . . . [a] sudden idea must have carried me back at one bound to something my patient had told me about a year and a half earlier. About two years previously the girl had become pregnant and, at his urgent entreaty, had procured an abortion. She had offered no great resistance to the suggestion of abortion, and had undergone the operation, which proved difficult owing to special cricumstances, with real heroism."

In commenting on this revelation, Reik said: "Now was it the words 'putting on flesh' in his story that roused the memory? How else could the latent meaning of the lover's quarrel have revealed itself to me? I could not tell, even though I were to repeat the story with the accuracy of a gramophone."

Reik has many case reports in his book depicting the art and magic of the "third ear" experience. He seems mystified by his own uncanny powers and reminds the reader at one point that therapists are not gods. Reik suggests in his writings that an effective therapist must have this sensitive "third ear" quality. Having a "third ear" is something like being born an artist. It is an artistic extrasensory ability that supposedly enables the therapist to detect the hidden beat, or rhythms, of the unconscious systems. Therapists have been promising for the last thirty or forty years that their particular treatment technology with its special "third ear" quality will "cure" the consumer of his mental health ailments. The solution to mental illness has been linked to special ways of listening, to unique communications, or to various profound interventions.

Therapists, relying on their clever but unproven techniques, have expected the various publics to accept their promises in good faith, despite the lack of evaluation and the many personal failures in the life-styles of caregivers; e.g., psychiatry has the highest suicide rate of any profession, caregivers have high divorce rates, and there are ever-increasing mental health problems occurring in the society.

In the last ten years, because of public pressure the first tentative attempts at evaluation have taken place—particularly in residential treatment facilities. Desperate to prove their worth and thus increase their resources, the mental health professionals have gone into the "body count" business. Good treatment has been equated with the number of patients discharged from treatment services. It has become a statistical fetish, especially for the naïve statistician, to report the number of patients entering a system, the average daily census (number of patients occupying beds), and the number of patients discharged. We would probably support the notion that body counts are superior to no evaluation at all; but unfortunately, reduced body counts have uncritically and automatically led to the simple-minded conclusion that fewer bodies in institutions mean proportionately less need for funds and staff. This is clearly a case where one body is not equal to another body.

We are suggesting that the field of mental health is highly subjective, capricious, and dominated by whims, mythologies, and public relations. In many ways it is a pop culture with endless fads but with no real substance. Listed below are a few of the many "ultimate solutions" that have emerged in the field of mental health during the last fifty years.

1. Bromides (a form of chemotherapy)
2. Convulsive therapies (shock treatments such as electric convulsive therapy, insulin therapy)
3. Psychoanalysis (one of many psychotherapeutic procedures)
4. Lobotomies (psychosurgery)
5. Tranquilizers (the most recent chemotherapy)
6. Transactional analysis (a recent form of psychotherapy)

It is the primary purpose of this book to inform the attentive layman and to help the various mental health "consumers" who participate in the operation of the mental health system. Unfortunately, we feel that most persons are still indoctrinated with an exotic, mystical, and romantic conception of mental health much like that presented in motion pictures such as *Spellbound* or *The Seventh Veil,* or in the writing of Reik (1946). Most people still think that mental health should be in the hands of experts. We are suggesting instead that institutionalizing mental health and identifying mental health with expert caregivers is antitherapeutic.

There are several themes and paradoxes in this last paragraph which we consider important, perhaps complicated, and to which we feel our readers should be sensitized. We do feel that it is important for the various disciplines to have experts and/or consultants. These experts are the explorers, information sources, "first aid" practitioners, risk takers, and conceptualizers. However, it becomes dangerous when these experts attempt to exclude consumers and publics as coparticipants. We think that the establishment of caste systems (patient versus therapist) in the human service areas (e.g., mental hospitals, schools, prisons, etc.) is particularly destructive. And it is clear that the belief that there will always be enough mental health therapists, prison rehabilitation workers, or teachers to meet the needs of the consumers and publics is delusional.

The experts locked into their miniature societies pull farther and farther out of orbit from the individuals and the institutions they are to serve. The training in the school systems becomes incongruent with the needs of employers. Prisons and mental hospitals do not prepare their residents for societal living. Treatment models seem to reflect the needs of the professional societies that create them.

Human service agencies have to be relinked to their constituencies. We have to find ways that will allow the community to become an equal partner in the human services consortium. We hope this book will help in this enterprise.

We will begin this task by attempting to describe and explain the major, or dominant, contemporary themes in mental health. It is the assumptions and implications of these models that result in many of the criticisms and investigations of the mental health consortium. We will present a classical theoretical position in order to establish a base position. Currently, there are modifying trends; but for purposes of communication, we will delineate the reasonably pure position.

## CURRENT CONCEPTIONS: THE MEDICAL-FREUDIAN MODEL

There are certain contemporary conceptions developed by the caregivers and accepted at face value by laymen. The primary focus of the field has been on abnormal behavior, or deviancy. It has been a core assumption of the experts that abnormal behavior, or mental illness, results from a disease process. That is, those behaviors considered to be abnormal, or deviant, are an expression of an internal disease (an intraorganismic process). This disease process is considered to be no different from any other disease. In this way schizophrenia and hysteria can take their places in the categories of diseases along with pneumonia, measles, diphtheria, etc.

Packaged with the traditional diseases, the mental health models functioned in the hospital-specialist-disease-cure system. Each new generation of mental health caregivers developed more elaborate diagnostic models, which typically meant a new generation of jargon. We have had gross poetic labels: schizophrenic reaction, chronic undifferentiated type; personality pattern disturbance, cyclothymic personality. A total and useless diagnostic system can be seen in the established document *Diagnostic and Statistical Manual of Mental Disorders.*

It has been assumed that when a person becomes mentally ill it helps to label him. Labeling, or diagnosing, is predicated on the notion that correct diagnosis leads to the proper treatment. The fact that Hollingshead and Redlich (1969) have demonstrated the absurdity of this position has done nothing to reduce the labeling process. All over America there are mental health specialists labeling persons called patients in an empty, meaningless ritual. Hollingshead and Redlich have demonstrated that mental health treatment is based more on race and socioeconomic status than on diagnostic categories. In every state in America when a person passes through the portals of the mental health establishment the diagnostic brand is firmly placed on the patient's psyche. There is no one who cannot be labeled.

In addition to the diagnosis, and in conjunction with the diagnostic process, it seemed important to establish a cause. We identified wicked mothers, incestuous fathers, strange blood chemistry, and unknown genetic defects. The search through time and through the various systems of the patient produced nothing of value. The fruitless search has done little to alter the operating systems of the specialists. For endless periods of time in hospitals and doctors' offices the eternal probe has continued. It has been the hope of the practitioners that eventually a Nobel Prize-winning scientist would discover a "cure" or a "vaccine" that would wipe out these dreaded "diseases." Until this "Dr. Arrowsmith" arrived on the scene, it would be the task of "super" elite therapists to practice their particular form of treatment.

We will later describe in detail how these specialists did their thing, awaited their messiah, and at the same time refused to alter their system to meet the overwhelming needs of their consumers. "Snake pits" formed, jails became overcrowded, mental health systems disintegrated, and therapists continued to march to the rhythm of their own needs. This is not the arrogance of the individual professional, but the arrogance of a system of professionals who feel that the mental health "industry" belongs to them.

Although the hospital-specialist-disease-cure system was a core pattern of many schools of thought, as a system it can probably best be understood by examining and describing the Freudian model. There is little question that Freud is the contemporary seminal force in mental health, and probably he has been the single most influential thinker in placing mental illness in the context of disease.

Freud assumed that all human beings in the process of growth pass through stages of development—psychosexual stages. Many other major thinkers in the field have followed this orientation: Erikson (1950), Klein (1932), Piaget (1932), Sullivan (1953), *et al.* The characteristics of these stages and the manner in which we move through them are determined by heredity and life experiences with the crucial people in our early life: mother, father, siblings, and the family constellation. It is believed that during each stage we arrive at a critical point, or crisis, which can be resolved in one of three ways: growth, fixation, or decline. Theoretically, good mental health is achieved by successfully working through or adapting to these stages, which results in an integrated personality.

A quick review of our environment makes it clear that most persons do not achieve the utopian integration called "normality." It is the contention of psychoanalysts that many growth issues particularly in reference to sex and hate are not resolved because of societal taboos and inhibitions. The individual who is unable to express certain feelings is forced to repress them— shove the unacceptable feelings into the "underground." This repression results in the construction of the unconscious system and the fixing of the individual at some earlier stage. This underground system and the early fixations become the main determiners of motivation, feelings, traits, and behavior.

It is essential to discuss the unconscious system in more detail because this is a cornerstone of the model. It is an accepted axiom of the Freudian system that the unconscious positions of the psyche cannot be controlled, regulated, or monitored by the conscious decision-making apparatus (the Executive Ego) of the individual. This is the theme that Freud utilized to place abnormal, or deviant, behavior in the context of physical illness, or disease. This particular axiom, that persons who performed in a deviant fashion were unable to interrupt their deviancy with their volitional system (the determinism and volitional issue), created a series of complex problems. If a person engages in sinful behavior, should he be held responsible? Should a person be placed in prison if he cannot control his behavior? Is mental illness different from a broken leg? Aren't all these failures outside the individual's control? The question of responsibility and consequences had to be rethought in detail if the individual was unable to determine his own destiny. This question has been a major catalytic force in twentieth-century permissiveness.

Freud identified a tyrannical and irrational task master that was not subject to the dimensions of time or place. Although the unconscious is the mainspring of action, this hidden portion of the psyche is immune to the everyday experiences of life and is not subject to modification by consequences. One could only communicate with the unconscious through the highly sophisticated technology of the mental health experts.

It is also a major axiom of the system that the unconscious always finds expression. If the expression is not direct or through sublimation (socially acceptable substitutive behavior), unconscious tensions appear as symptoms, unacceptable behavior, and/or maladaptive defense mechanisms; tics, slips of the tongue, hallucinations, criminal behavior, etc. It is out of this axiom that we have assumed that to alter human behavior significantly, we must first alter the unconscious system (the cause). Altering the conscious system, removing the symptom, and changing behavior are seen as only temporary measures; the forces of the unconscious will again resume their deterministic tyranny. For many years this theme resulted in the neglect of a variety of effective "first aid" methods: hypnosis, behavior modification, and milieu therapy.

From this model which focused on the unconscious, new technology and a new profession developed. The process of diagnosis and treatment is considered terribly complicated and lengthy. The therapist has to find accessibility to this deeply buried unconscious system. Out of this need has developed a therapeutic and diagnostic technology that is utilized in an attempt to communicate with the unconscious systems: free association, interpretation of dreams, interpretation of everyday pathology, projective techniques, and the analysis of detailed case histories. These processes are time-consuming, require considerable expertise, and are difficult to evaluate. In fact, there are probably only a handful of persons in the nation who can deliver these services adequately.

The focus of the treatment is to search the past through an intense relationship with the therapist. If the reader would like to understand this process in detail, he should read the works of Freud (1949), Glover (1968), and Reich (1933). Unless the therapy is managed properly (and how one determines that is a real puzzle), the patient's existential reality is lost in an outpatient career that might well endure ad infinitum. In effect, the patient is recruited into the mental health network and frequently breaks from his former adaptive style.

The professionals who manage this system are, of course, the psychoanalysts. These are, indeed, the "super" elite therapists. Their post high school training is almost endless. It is certainly not atypical for an analyst to receive his credentials in his late thirties or in his forties. He emerges as the explorer, advocate, and expert of the unconscious, the true "Land of Oz." As an aside, it is worth noting how often experts receive their blessing from other experts, in their own image. It does seem that expertism has many built-in "incestuous," nepotism-like themes.

As in all disease models, psychoanalysts judge patients in regard to their prognosis. In this case a good prognosis is based on the client or patient, depending upon socioeconomic level, achieving a "normal" behavior pattern (a cure) by means of the psychoanalytical techniques. Those patients who are not able to function within the psychoanalytical system are considered to have a poor prognosis. In the eyes of caregivers that probably means that such patients are inferior, unintelligent, and inarticulate—definitely of a lower "class" or "caste."

The clients who do have a good prognosis have very specific qualities. They must be sufficiently tied into the cash economy that they can afford a significant cash outlay—a minimum of two thousand dollars per year. This usually indicates well-developed occupational skills, a "successful" marriage, and/or wealthy relatives. The therapy model demands an articulate person who is able to mature through this type of experience. A typical client is middle class, verbal, most likely a female, above average in intelligence, and diagnosed neurotic. When you consider the entire distribution of persons seeking and needing help, only a trickle meet the requirements that result in their being considered good prognostic risks.

Most therapeutic systems in the twentieth century have adopted this medical notion of labeling those persons not responding to their therapeutic procedures as being grave therapeutic risks. We have here another example of the middle class developing models that support their way of life as being right, proper, and healthy, and lower-class norms as inappropriate and unhealthy. Schools honor the A and B students (primarily the middle class); all other students suffer and lose dignity through their school careers. Personnel officers evaluate candidates on the basis of the occupant of the current position (middle-class persons). Whyte (1956) does an excellent job of describing the nepotism model in industry. The prognostic model classifies with the school model and the personnel-practice model. We build systems that support the majority power group and build barriers against the other groups through concepts like prognosis. We have a situation where mild mental illness is middle class and serious mental illness is lower class and appropriate for institutionalization—state hospitals are occupied primarily by lower-class persons.

Patients who do not have the "good sense" to respond to our treatment models find themselves in the continuous process of expulsion (exile). It is not the therapeutic system that is chastised so much as the individual who does not respond.

The analytical process generally takes anywhere from several years to an interminable period. The time dimension is an unknown factor. Freud (1950) in one of his last works wrote of the interminable analytical process. If one takes into consideration the few analysts available—there are currently approximately two thousand in the United States—the time necessary to complete the analysis, and the enormous potential consumer population, we are obviously confronted by serious logistic problems.

If we are to bring together in summary the Medical-Freudian position, it would seem that behavioral deviance is safely lodged in the category of a "disease." It is assumed that the causal factors are the result of early experiences. The search for causes and the treatment process itself take place in a dyadic relationship (therapist and client). The treaters are highly trained but few in number. It is not unfair to say that the successful consumers in this model are miniature copies of the therapist and in a sense highly trained by society for this role. The ultimate goal of this process is to produce the "Dr. Arrowsmith" who will discover a "cure" and win his second Nobel prize.

Possibly the worst evil of this system is the closed invariant aspect of the model. The professionals, despite the fact that they only serve an infinitesimal portion of the potential consumer market continue in their traditional model and tout their system as the solution to the problems of mental illness. The needs of the system and the professionals become the organizing force of the model. The many potential mental health consumers who do not fit the model are considered bad prognostic risks and are extruded. Their needs do not seem to have sufficient validity to alter the model or to create new models that will serve the "poor prognosis" consumer.

It is not the purpose of this book to assault the Medical-Freudian model per se. We are willing to accept the position that this approach has validity for a small group of clients who want to play this game, even though there is little evidence to support this position, its implications for the society, the attitudes communicated to the attentive publics, and the power of these influential groups to lay their imprint on all caregivers and the entire distribution of consumers.

It is a major task of this book not only to examine prevailing therapies but to understand the institutional impact of the model. It is our contention that most treatment results from institutional change and not from the specific therapy. We would predict that psychoanalysis will be evaluated more for its permissive impact on the society than for the few patients who have been treated or for the few analysts who have become famous and wealthy. We will explore the alternative concept of "treatment through institutional change" in Chapter III. A more technical understanding of the process can be found in papers by Fisher (1965b); Fisher, Mehr, and Truckenbrod (1971a, 1971b); Jones, McGee, and Grant (1952); Cumming and Cumming (1962); Mowrer (1962); and Hansell (1968).

The challenge to the Medical-Freudian position will allow us to identify a number of the "great issues" to which care-givers, attentive publics, and consumers must address them-selves. In the next chapter we will examine the contribution of the Medical-Freudian game plan to the collapse of an agency (a "critical mass" situation).

# II

# A "Critical Mass" Situation

The focus of this case history is on the authors' agency, a large, public, residential state hospital. In this chapter we will examine the "decline and fall" of this mental health facility; in fact, we approach "death." We refer to this "decline and fall" process as a "critical mass" situation. We first heard the term "critical mass" used in the social science context by Harold Visotsky, M.D., former director of the Department of Mental Health in Illinois.

Although the concept "critical mass" can be explained only in slightly technical terminology, it is a useful analogy and should be briefly explained. The concept "critical mass" refers to a general notion in nuclear engineering that has relevance both denotatively and connotatively for our own field of mental health. In nuclear engineering it concerns the minimum amount of radioactive material needed to sustain a chain reaction. All radioactive material decomposes because of an inherent instability in the configuration of the nucleus. The decomposition, or emission of neutrons and other atomic particles, is, in fact, what makes a particular element or isotope radioactive. Under normal conditions, decomposition takes place at an orderly, extremely precise rate. When enough radioactive material gets together, the neutrons from the decomposing atoms start to interact with other atoms, causing them in turn to decompose. The neutrons from these strike the nucleus of other atoms and a chain reaction is set in process. Of the two types of chain reaction processes, controlled and uncontrolled, controlled reactions are used for the purpose of generating energy in the form of heat, whereas in any uncontrolled nuclear chain reaction, the process is rapid and creates huge amounts of energy in a very short time. This is, of course, how an atomic bomb operates.

There seems to be a basic analogue to this nuclear engineering concept in mental health delivery systems as well as in societal systems in general. Static systems (those unresponsive to basic needs) that continue to utilize traditional or stereotypical responses to pressing demands quickly become overloaded by their input processes, eventually reaching a chain reaction level. The "critical mass" of the large, public, residential facilities such as ours has been the enormous numbers of patients demanding services; however, just as "critical mass" in nuclear engineering is dependent on a variety of factors, so "critical mass" in social sciences is linked to a number of variables.

The following quotation from Moore (1963), although not written in the context of the "critical mass," articulates portions of the concept very well.

Yet if the contemporary world is not uniformly chaotic, there are complexities in social change that are likely to manifest themselves as *tensions* and *strains*. Persistent patterns in one field of action may eventually collide with trends in another—for example, the persistent pattern that impels nearly everyone to go to work at the same hour in the morning may be increasingly inconsistent with urban growth, the resulting strains being reflected in overloaded transportation facilities and traffic congestion. Trends that are relatively impervious to attempts to alter them may offset deliberate planning—for example, trends in birth rate may be out of phase with respect to plans for improving schools. Slow and simple changes may intersect with rapid and complex transformations—for example, the

steady rate of economic growth through private invest-
ment may be inadequate to meet sudden and complex
changes in national defense needs and foreign aid policy.

Although one cannot accurately quantify "critical mass" situations in the social sciences, we believe that decomposition and
subsequent instabilities do develop in social systems which cannot meet the needs of their various consumers and publics.
This failure of mental health agencies to meet the needs of
consumers and publics can result in a "critical mass" configuration. The eleven points listed below are characteristic of such
configurations.

1. Staff develops pessimism, apathy, and a sense of despair.
2. The quality of staff, measured by the standards of the
   particular period, declines.
3. The residential population significantly increases, reaching a point where treatment is no longer possible.
4. The staff-to-patient ratio declines.
5. The highest quality staff turns over most rapidly.
6. The primary *service goals* of the agency are minimized
   and professional staff focuses on secondary functions
   such as training.
7. The agency receives less of the budget pie, and physical
   plant and equipment increasingly deteriorate.
8. Staff remaining in the system do not have the competency to utilize existing therapeutic modalities.
9. The number of treatment programs declines, and the
   caregivers become increasingly more involved in maintenance and custodial duties.
10. There is an increasing tendency to extrude, or exile, pa-
    tients. The community, unable to manage patients,
    quickly exiles them to residential facilities. Programs
    within the facility are unable to manage the patients and
    force them down the ladder to more regressed wards.
11. Continuity of treatment disappears; i.e., patients are
    transferred, the staff transfers, but there is no opportunity

to develop appropriate communications and therapeutic links between the previous caregivers and the new caregivers.

Our own agency developed these eleven characteristics.

The examination, monitoring, and evaluation of mental health facilities are done basically in the context of the Medical-Freudian model. Agencies are evaluated in terms of the number of physicians, the number of other professionals, the cleanliness of the buildings, the number of fire extinguishers, the quantity of traditional therapy, etc. The system pressures administrators of mental health facilities to invest their resources in activities highly valued in the Medical-Freudian model. When a state hospital, with its limited resources, is being prepared for an accreditation visit, the priorities shift dramatically. During a period beginning at least six months prior to the visitation, agencies must shift their resources from patient care to record-keeping, form preparation, and "super" housekeeping.

Even as we are in the process of preparing this book, our agency is beleaguered by a Senate investigative committee, and our primary problem, forgetting personalities, is communication. The committee members arrived at our agency with the traditional hospital image in the back of their heads. They looked for the antiseptic hospital, the physician in white coat treating a diseased patient, the nurse in white ministering to her poor charge. They compared us to their inner images of hospitals, university mental health facilities, and the many television physicians such as Dr. Welby; and we of course found ourselves lacking.

For a variety of reasons, mental health caregivers have been seriously deficient in educating their various publics on the difference in service models, the impact of different-size population groups, and the variety of different human problems that need to be serviced. Our attentive publics seldom realize that if all caregivers were to provide Mayo brothers' type of services for all mental health patients in the society, the expense would exceed the national defense budget. Not only would the cost soar, but it would be impossible to obtain or train sufficient staff to participate in this vast enterprise. We will examine a few dollar figures to make our point. On any one day the Department of Mental Health in Illinois has an inpatient census of around 25,000 patients. This does not include the huge number of patients who enter the system each year or the astronomical number of outpatients served.

Utilizing just this 25,000 figure, we will make our point. Assuming that we want to provide basic room, board, and daily care similar to that provided by the Riggs Foundation, the Menningers, or Chestnut Lodge, we are talking about a $100 per day figure. This means that we would be spending $2,500,000 per day on basic care for patients (25,000 patients multiplied by $100). If we multiply this figure by 365 to estimate the annual cost, we find that the figure for simple daily care for the year would be $912,500,000. This figure alone is about three times greater than the entire mental health budget for Illinois for the entire year. If one were to include the entire patient population, the therapy models, and physical plants at the level of the famous private agencies, the mental health budget for Illinois alone would run to many billions, probably the equivalent of the entire state budget of seven and a half billion dollars.

Even if it were the consensus that we should go the giant expenditure route, it is vital to realize that the famous private institutions have not in any way substantiated their effectiveness even for the populations they have served. The facts are that no caregiving system has ever been effectively evaluated. One can no more say that psychoanalysis is better than any other therapy system than that one religion is superior to another religion. To further confound issues, there is absolutely no evidence to prove that one therapist is more effective than another therapist. However, these facts are ignored by caregivers, consumers, and attentive publics alike. It is a societal delusion that therapy is a science and that through the scientific method we can arrive at truths about this process. Probably the greatest paradox is that legislators and accrediting agencies evaluate agencies against a nonexistent treatment ideal.

As we indicated, in this chapter we will describe the "decline and fall" of a state hospital over a period of three decades (1930–1957). It is our contention that the major factors in the collapse of the institution, the factors that caused the "critical mass" situation, were the mythologies, power struggles, and deliberate deceptions regarding the problems of those persons labeled as mentally ill.

## The Golden Age of Investigation (1930–1945)

This was the era of the professional in a white coat looking at patients through microscopes, Rorschachs, and X-rays with the hope of discovering the cause of mental illness. It was a time of great expectancy. Dr. Philip Bower, chief psychologist at Elgin State Hospital from 1954 to 1970, in a personal communication described this expectancy very well. "There was, for instance, the hope that substances relating to psychiatric illness could be found in the bodies of the patients, that drugs could 'cure' or that the illness could be so well understood and documented by an elite group of intellectuals that therapy could be prescribed precisely."

At the dawning of this era the patient population at our agency was around 3,000 and the available staff including housekeepers, maintenance workers, dietary workers, etc., consisted of around 950. In addition to the 3,000 inpatients, around 150 new patients were brought in each month. The ineffectiveness of the discharge procedure can be seen by the additional 1,500 patients that accumulated in the hospital by the end of the era—at that time we had around 4,500 patients.

The staff did attempt to mimic the classic giant expenditure hospital model. Although most of the patients were brought to the hospital involuntarily—the prison model—the staff carefully attempted to evaluate, diagnose, prescribe, and treat each patient for a "disease"—the hospital model. It was the essence of what Szasz (1961) describes as "paternalism." It was service that we were providing for the patient's "good." This is the same evil rationalization used to justify slavery, mistreating children, and violating the rights of most minority groups.

The stupidity of the system was not yet obvious, because most persons entering the hospital were discharged. The staff and the public did not realize that they were accumulating a residual population of one hundred per year—this was to be a problem of the future. The agency at that time met all the accrediting procedures and was seldom assaulted by legislative investigating committees. It was congruent with cultural mythologies.

There were several factors that made the mental hospital situation more viable during this era; i.e., factors that kept the body count down. During economically depressed periods, there is a reduced tendency for persons to label themselves or for other persons to label them mentally ill. In effect, you have fewer potential patients arriving at the door. At the same time it was possible to attract staff of a higher caliber to participate in the patients' everyday milieu. This was a more intelligent and more concerned staff than we found in mental hospitals in the '40s and '50s. As a result of the WPA (Works Projects Administration) there was a reconstitution of the physical environment by the addition of a number of new buildings. These factors resulted in making the hospital more tolerable.

The caregivers, feeling that they were in control of the situation and working in the image of "Dr. Arrowsmith," developed a series of awesome weapons to treat their patients: varieties of lobotomies, Metrazol shock, insulin therapy, electric convulsive therapy, injections of sulfur and oil. During this fifteen-year period, we witnessed man's most protracted onslaught against the central nervous system. This was, of course, being done for the good of the patient. The therapists, without meaningful evaluation, reported great successes and stood humbly by, waiting for Nobel prizes. As an aside, it should be noted that most of the great therapy techniques of the era have either disappeared from the marketplace or are moving toward oblivion.

Beginning with World War II, the failure of the system became clear, although some said the decomposition was temporary. It was assumed that after the war the hospital staff would return and the investigation would continue. The excitement of the war era did not allow anyone to examine the decade of the '30s to see that it was a failure. It was not until the next era that the grotesque and perverse quality of the medical model for state hospital patients could be observed.

## THE DECLINE AND FALL OF A MENTAL HEALTH RACKET
### (1945–1957)

It became apparent in the late '40s that solutions to the problems labeled "mental illness" had not been found. The many "cures" such as lobotomies and convulsive therapies were not working. The alleged "elite" therapists were gone from the state hospitals, and they were not returning after the war. The therapies that they reported as successful in the 1930's seemed to have a declining effectiveness. However, the loss of staff and the declining effectiveness did not seem to have any impact on the style of the hospital. Everyone continued to operate in the hospital-specialist-disease-cure approach. The staff continued to utilize the same clinical tools: staff meetings, sophisticated diagnostic techniques, prescriptive therapies, and prognostic evaluations. With approximately 1,000 staff persons, most of whom were not considered professionals or therapists, over

6,000 patients in residence, and with 250 new patients arriving at the door each month, few patients could receive the benefit of the complex clinical-services system. The ultimate absurdity and futility of this model could be seen in the staff meetings held each morning. Seventy-five percent of the "purported" treatment staff would gather in the conference room to examine thoroughly one "classic" patient—shades of the Golden Age of Investigation! These staff meetings would last from 8:00 A.M. to 10:30 A.M. Those in attendance would typically continue an informal discussion of the case until lunchtime. The patients "staffed" were atypical in that they were the "interesting" cases, types seen in the private systems, and not like the mass numbers of patients piled up in the back ward "snake pits."

The content of the staff meetings would focus on those factors which contributed to the individual's mental illness, the diagnosis, the deep inner Freudian dynamics, treatment under ideal circumstances, etc. The focus was on factors beyond hospital resources and expertise. The staff, buried in a deep dream state, continued these irrelevant staff meetings for at least ten years beyond the time that they had any meaning to the system. The entire enterprise was typical of the times. Training events of the classical Medical-Freudian model were the opium that allowed staff to continue to tolerate their dreary work experience. Patients who fit the pattern of the Medical-Freudian model received most of the action. As the staff sat through these intensive clinical investigations, the hospital became increasingly loaded with patients. All attempts to treat patients, except for the select few at the reception wards, disappeared.

The inner hospital literally regressed into a "snake pit." The continued application of the traditional treatment model, patient on a couch, demanding large numbers of highly professional clinicians who were unavailable, led to the moral abandonment of large numbers of patients. Even if the traditional model had proved successful for the target population of the state hospital, there would never have been enough staff to provide services through this model. However, most patients were abandoned because they had been designated as having a poor prognosis for available treatment systems. The staff, probably out of guilt, became desperate about preventing patients from riding the assembly line into the back wards. Since most professional staff members, the "therapists," were placed in the reception wards to prevent flow into the inner "hell," the back wards were denied any possibility of upgrading. The phenomenon included soaring ward populations, little treatment of any sort, an overriding preoccupation on the part of the back ward caretakers with hygiene, orderliness, and the prevention of acting out fantasies through repressive measures (law and order policies without justice). New patients were held at the reception wards as long as possible, resulting in these wards' becoming crowded, thus reducing treatment effectiveness even at the point of maximal service delivery. Vicious circles that drained staff effectiveness were created in all sections of the hospital.

We will take a temporary detour to aid the reader further in comprehending subsequent events. Patients coming into residential care, particularly in state hospitals, are locked up because they have violated (or might violate) the cultural mores, laws, rules, etc. In legal terminology the process is described as occurring "if that person, as a result of such mental illness, is reasonably expected at the time the determination is being made or within a reasonable time thereafter to intentionally or unintentionally physically injure himself or other persons, or is unable to care for himself so as to guard himself from physical injury or to provide for his own physical needs." This quotation is the basic rationale for committing a person involuntarily to a mental hospital under the Mental Health Code, 1968, in the State of Illinois.

The basic theory of hospitalization includes several assumptions. It is first *assumed* that there can come a time in a person's life when his decision-making ability can no longer be trusted—this is equivalent to mental illness. It is *assumed* that we have the expertise to identify this condition and treat this "disorder" through the medical model. The ultimate paternalistic assumption states that when a person has his volition disturbed, we, the caregivers, know what is best for him and should take control of his behavior. *We can state without reservation that there is not one shred of evidence to support any of these assumptions.* We cannot reliably predict homicide or suicide—that is apparent from every edition of every daily paper. Further, we have no technology for interfering with or preventing these processes from taking place. The high rate of suicide among psychiatrists is evidence of this.

The staffs have ignored their lack of information and technology. They continue to operate on the Medical-Freudian premises. They attempt to solve the problem by identifying the "disease process" that disrupted the decision-making system. They have generated a variety of factors that they consider causal forces of the alleged "disease process." In response to their alleged theories of cause, they have developed the multitude of intervention systems cited earlier: convulsive therapies, chemotherapies, couch therapies, hydrotherapy, and packs.

The increased body counts made it clear that we were not being successful in returning patients to the community. By 1955 our agency had an average daily census of almost 7,000 patients. An acceptable bed standard for an agency of our size is about 2,000. Certainly by this time it was apparent, even to the administrators, that we were not being successful in our quest. As this process of decomposition continued, responsible authority became increasingly sensitive about the inner anarchy. However, their sensitivity did not make them more adaptive or result in new delivery systems. Instead the administrators leaned more heavily on a security and cleanliness model. Administrators learned that they were *not* punished for *failure* to treat. Punishment for administrators was meted out for acts of commission regardless of motivation—it was important never to rock the boat. Afraid of criticism, administrators left decision-making in the hands of "super" experts. In our agency three men, all in administrative positions, infrequent visitors to the wards, made most formal decisions regarding the operation of the hospital and the fate of the patients. Even though these men had the best credentials, the superintendent felt he had to review all their decisions. As an aside, it should be noted that most superintendents who survived the era were cautious and timid men. Assuming that the credentialed people had the wisdom to make appropriate judgments, they were overwhelmed by the size of the task—the vicious circle. If any of the administrators became ill or went on vacation, the already staggering system would approach collapse. Important decisions would be delayed or never made, and patients who might have been quickly moved through the system were held and institutionalized.

The accumulation of patients left staff with two alternative conclusions. They could conclude either that the system, or model, was ineffective or that patients were profoundly "sick" people with an extremely poor prognosis. Administrators had no difficulty accepting the latter conclusion. Under these circumstances treatment would have to be long, careful, complicated, and deep. The remainder of the logic model is not difficult to simulate. Such a treatment model required highly trained therapists. There were few such therapists available in state departments of mental health. Therefore the resources should be organized around those patients with the most potential resources—good prognosis. The remainder of the patients received few if any services.

The patients who did not respond to the caregiving models made available in the agency were seen as a hopeless, helpless, and contemptible group. If they would not assume responsibility and volitional control through the humane Medical-Freudian model, they would, of course, have to live in a society that controlled them. Miniature authoritarian societies, jail-like, developed to assume the responsibility and care for these people. Staff took over the responsibility for the lives of these patients. Patients were robbed of their volition. All decision-making was to be in the hands of elite specialists with high-level academic credentials who could make the crucial life decisions and be above suspicion. There were never enough funds for the experts, so informally the society was organized by the lowest-paid caretakers who were actually on the scene.

In the late '40s and early '50s our agency regressed to its nadir. We had failed to live up to the standards of the existing models, e.g., general hospitals, private practice, and small, exclusive private hospitals. Not being able to achieve the level of expectancies of these models, we lost our hospital accreditation, we lost our residency programs, and we saw a good deal of the remaining professional staff dwindle away. Despite the public stripping, regardless of the failure of the system, and in spite of any rescue attempts by outside experts and universities, most administrators wanted to hold the line. There stood the hospital locked in its impotent posture, spinning wheels in quicksand.

To add fuel to this fire, the Department of Mental Health in the early '50s built a training and research hospital to help us find a way out of the quicksand. Although it would seem almost impossible to believe, the hospital was built in the classic private agency model. The hospital became a training ground for psychiatrists to enter private practice. The department was actually subsidizing the future wealthy psychiatrist, while most of the state hospitals were quickly and quietly sinking into the mire. Adding insult to injury, this training and research hospital stole many good employees from state hospitals, extruded its many patient failures to the state hospitals, and obviously looked down its nose at the employees in state hospitals.

As we passed through the '30s, '40s, and '50s, there were many obvious issues that we ignored. The false logic and stupidity of the system seems beyond belief. It does appear clear in perspective that the primary task of state hospitals, and perhaps of most caregivers, is to serve the disadvantaged person. In our current idiom these patients are considered the "high risk" patients. That is, these are persons with poor educational development, little in the way of career patterns, a poor tie-in with the cash economy, not much in the way of intimate personal relationships, and a minimal social network (obviously little in the way of social resources). These are persons who, under stress, quickly demonstrated those characteristics which we assume require hospitalization: identity confusion, role confusion, homicidal or suicidal patterns, hallucinations, etc. The paradox of the '30s, '40s, and '50s is that although these were the chief consumers of the state hospital, they were universally considered poor treatment risks. They frequently became our permanent boarders.

The plight of our "high risk" consumers and potential consumers can probably best be understood from the sociological perspective. Their life situation limited them to a minimal number of options. They could possibly maintain themselves at a marginal level indefinitely—accommodate themselves to an unacceptable life situation. They could attempt to link themselves into the mainstream of society via inadequate educational systems, almost nonexistent career patterns, and unavailable work opportunities. They could, of course, and many did, pursue a criminal career and attempt to utilize this style of life as a career pattern. Finally, when these other options were unacceptable or unavailable, the "high risk" individual could select or be pushed into deviance (mental illness) as a way of reacting to his everyday stress. The state hospitals were and are primarily populated by this latter group. These "high risk" patients come or are brought to our door to escape the stress patterns in their lives—possibly as a "cop-out." The patients took on those patterns of behavior which are the passports into mental hospitals.

These clients came to our "ports of entry"—variously called

diagnostic centers, reception wards, and intake wards. No one was refused entry or given constructive alternatives (deflected). These intake wards were, of course, modeled on those of general hospitals: physical examinations, laboratory work, development of diagnosis, and development of treatment plan. In every sense these were the best wards in the hospital.

The staff in the context of the medical model attempted to examine the inner problems of the disadvantaged person. There was an attempt to find some intraorganismic problem—neurological, chemical, or psychological—that might be causing the asocial or antisocial problems. If the experts felt they could define the cause, sophisticated intervention procedures were attempted in order to eradicate the problem. This brought the patient to a "crossroads" decision. To him, recovery meant a reasonably early discharge to his previous existence, with the possible beginning of a recidivism pattern. The failure to respond to treatment meant the acceptance of patienthood and the descent into the "snake pit." The patient would leave behind his previous social network and would be recruited into this mental health network with all its consequences for behavior.

Utilizing this model, we recruited 4,000 new members into our hospital society in a period of 20 years. The type of clients who were brought into the state hospital were particularly vulnerable to the impact of the institutionalizing process. The patients declined with the institution—or perhaps, in a complementary fashion, the institution declined with the patients. The hospital set up a negative career ladder that moved in only one direction. "Success" in this career meant moving from the reception ward to the most regressed "snake pit." Although the professional staff with their fantasies gave the intake wards their special flavor, the remainder of the hospital was given form and style by the caretakers and the patients.

The patients found these "back ward ghettos" to be a milieu in which they could adapt without much internal or external stress. The built-in reward-and-punishment system supported the patient career. Patients and families had to learn that once you went into these custodial wards your prognosis was hopeless. The built-in expectancy was that the patient had become a "lifer." Although professionals assume that crisis conditions precede growth, those factors which create crises were eradicated in the back ward. Hope of rescue, expectancies, aspirations, dreams, and fantasies were totally crushed in this debasing, punitive environment.

Patients who became excited were seen as "bad" or dangerous. The only time the psychiatrist was called into these areas was when a patient became disturbed. At that point the various restraint systems, such as disturbed wards, chemotherapy, and hydrotherapy, were brought forward to crush the excitement or crisis. This refusal to tolerate or work with excitement was interesting since it was part of the belief of the time that excitement was a sign of a good prognosis. It was actually evident that this type of environment supported only those behavioral patterns which were associated with chronicity, apathy, and hopelessness.

We will present some anecdotal material that expresses the built-in value system which led to the "critical mass" configuration.

ANECDOTE I

It was assumed, of course, that patients were not responsible for their behavior. Because patients could not control themselves they were not allowed to use knives and forks with their meals. All sharp instruments were considered dangerous. (It is difficult to find an employee who can report from personal experience an instance of a patient attacking another person with a sharp instrument.)

This policy led patients to eat certain items with their hands, e.g., tough meat. It wasn't long before employees and visitors were describing patients as eating like animals. The eating with their hands was seen as part of their "disease." Eventually this eating style became the typical behavior.

ANECDOTE II

Patient clothing rooms were set up with a monitor at the door to prevent thefts. If a patient wanted to change clothing, he had to get permission from the monitor to obtain his own clothing. If the monitor was bothered too frequently, which meant that his job became more difficult, he would give the "customer" a "hard time." Soon adaptive patients stopped asking for changes of clothing, which meant they began to look dirty and were described as messy in appearance. Eventually this became the ward expectancy.

ONE-LINE ANECDOTES OF DEHUMANIZATION

Patients were not allowed to handle their own funds.
Patients were not allowed to interact with the opposite sex.
Patients were limited in their movement away from the ward.
Patients were not allowed to participate in making decisions about their own destiny.

IMPLICATIONS

In summary and in retrospect, we are saying that the greater portion of the deviance seen in our agency was a reflection of the social system and not a function of an inner disease process. We are saying that it was important to supplement the Medical-Freudian orientation with public health and human service models. The failure to recognize the needs of the time caused our agency to stagger toward collapse—"critical mass." In the next chapter we will see the agency's attempt to reconstitute itself. This attempt to reorganize led to new concepts of service and subsequently to new ideologies and philosophies.

# III

## "Treatment Through Institutional Change"

In this chapter we will examine the attitudes, forces, and causes that began to "turn our agency around." We would like to make an immediate disclaimer. When we say "turn our agency around," we do not mean that we created a Camelot. What we do mean, very simply, is that we brought about a major reduction in the body count, improved the quality of our staff, increased our options for services and placement, reduced length of stay, upgraded our physical plant and equipment. The changes that took place were part of a process. Staff began an examination and working through of their attitudes that allowed them to escape the deep and controlling assumptions of the Medical-Freudian model. This was not a single-day or even a single-year event. It was something that began in the late '50s, is continuing through the present, and we hope will continue into the future. In presenting this chapter, not only are we focusing on the changing institution but also we want the reader to be sensitive to the process of staff members working through their implicit and explicit feelings about the Medical-Freudian model.

We should begin this analysis of change with an assessment of staff attitudes, particularly that of the direct care staff. By direct care staff, we mean those persons who actually serve patients in a face-to-face relationship. These staff persons were aware that the treatment systems in our agency were failing, and they were embarrassed by the "snake pits," for which they felt some responsibility. These employees felt little emotional loyalty to the failing treatment models and in this sense had a high threshold for change. However, it should be noted that for persons in our culture it is extremely difficult to escape intellectually the assumptions and the operational network of the Medical-Freudian model. These concepts seemed to be deeply embedded in our thinking processes.

After World War II, it was no longer fashionable to ignore and discriminate against the disadvantaged. Sociologists, urban planners, and ecologists began to point out the failures of the cities in meeting the needs of the ghetto populations. In the middle '50s and early '60s these same critics began pointing their fingers directly toward the mental hospitals. People were becoming impatient with all bureaucratic and institutional failures. It became less fashionable to examine the inner problems of disadvantaged persons. There seemed to be little to gain by saying that a person was lazy or unmotivated, or to make a prognostic statement about the individual. Our attention was directed toward social systems, institutions, and the environment. The critics were saying that if we were to help these disadvantaged persons, we would have to do so by altering the environment and not the inner man. Martin (1955), Barton (1959), Goffman (1961), and Wing (1962) suggested that many of those characteristics we ascribed to psychiatric illness were a function of the existing social systems in the mental hospitals. That is, the hospitals were literally making their residents "sicker."

For years, on the basis of what was good for the residents (good old paternalism), patients had been relieved of personal belongings, separated from their families, cut off from jobs and responsibility. Each patient was isolated from the crucial attachments of his existence and placed into a vague,

unstructured, and deviant environment. The patient, robbed
of his past, had little alternative but to take on the identity
of patienthood (a new career). The social critics were raising a crucial question: What part of the mental illness process
was attributable to an inner disease process and to what extent was the strange behavior in hospitals related to the pressures of the institution?

The introduction of a new treatment modality played an
important role in setting the stage for change within our
agency. In the early 1950's, when the hospital's functioning
was approaching its nadir, the new chemotherapy of tranquilizers was introduced into our agency. It was *assumed* by
many, at that time, that this new chemotherapy would "cure"
mental illness. In this frame of reference, it had a negative
impact on the system. It renewed the Nobel prize illusion:
i.e., it reactivated the belief that all unacceptable behavior was
a result of a "disease process" and that eventually a caregiver
would discover a "cure" for the "disease." It reactivated the
descendants of the "Golden Age" with all their wishes and
illusions. It seems important for many persons to believe that
deviance results from an inner "disease process" rather than
to believe that it is an expression of cultural system problems.
For example, a community develops an addiction problem
with its adolescents, but instead of examining characteristics
of their community that might have caused such problems,
they call for experts who, they hope, will solve the problem in
regard to the teen-agers' "disease process." The community
goes untouched.

From our perspective, the emergence of the tranquilizers
was important as a patient-management technique. It changed
staff and patient attitudes and affect regarding those behaviors
which we considered to fall in the categories of mental illness.
It allowed staff to witness dramatic changes of behavior in
so-called hopeless patients in brief periods of time. This aided
staff to feel more optimistic about the caregiving process and

to witness change without long, complicated intervention systems.

Caregivers now felt some competence in managing the patients. They were much less frightened by the acting out of hostile residents. Employees did not have to be utilized in purely guarding and security roles. It became possible to reduce the number of disturbed wards and to eliminate the more severe somatic techniques.

We should say that at the time we were not sensitized to the sociological implications of the various tranquilizers. Our minds were still locked in to the notion that the problems of mental illness were to be totally resolved by a great clinical discovery. Discussions at our agency concerning the tranquilizers revolved around their curative impact.

We should make another detour at this point and present several disclaimers. The reader is aware that much of the focus of this book is on the impact of the external stimuli—social systems, sociopsychological factors, sociological systems, etc. This does not mean that we are disregarding the inner man. We have no doubt that what you do inside the individual, whether it is through the input of chemicals or through psychoanalysis, does play a role in the behavior of the individual. However, we feel that the focus has been too one-sided in regard to the importance of the inner man, and we feel that a counterbalance is required. This book is not focusing on damaging other systems. It is really an effort to provide new options.

We want to present the second disclaimer in regard to the tranquilizers. We do not mean to imply that the chemical effect of the drugs was irrelevant. However, we do feel that it is important to tease out the impact of social change from the chemical factors.

We would like to give an example of the confounding relationship between the inner impact of the treatment and the influence of the environment. In the 1930's, insulin shock therapy was introduced into our hospital. Typical of such programs, and because of the need to regulate diet, a special ward was set aside for patients who were to receive insulin shock therapy. This resulted in the creation of a special staff-patient community for the delivery of the treatment. As was typical of pilot projects, the best physical space and the best employees were utilized. The early evaluations reported a "cure" rate of 95 percent, which probably meant discharge from the hospital. It was *assumed* for a number of years that the insulin therapy was the important agent in recovery. As the years passed, the insulin therapy continued, but the energy and the resources put into the community diminished. By the early '60s, the insulin community was gone, and at the time insulin therapy was abandoned, the reported "cures" had reached the zero level.

During the 1950's a number of influential writers began to question key assumptions in the traditional mental health models. We will focus on two such thinkers, Dr. O. H. Mowrer and Dr. Thomas Szasz, because they had the most influential impact on our agency, and because both of these men have had to do a lot of their own working through in regard to the issues of mental health and the Medical-Freudian model. We will present their thinking only where it touches on issues relevant to our own position. Although we think that we are presenting their positions accurately, we are interpreting, and this does mean that there is some potential for bias. We should also point out that our position is not totally congruent with Mowrer or Szasz, nor are Mowrer and Szasz completely congruent in their orientation. However, there are some key themes that did influence our agency personnel and are integral to this book.

Mowrer (1962, 1966a, 1966b) has written extensively in regard to his position on mental health. He has pointed out in the above-cited papers and in personal communication that his initial orientation in therapy was psychoanalytical. It is worth noting how many famous caregivers, e.g., Jung, Adler, Rank, Stekel, Szasz, Mowrer, *et al.*, started out from a psychoanalytical orbit and then moved into a new and independent orbit. It raises an interesting question. If so many sophisticated thinkers can arrive at so many different personality and treatment models, are we dealing with a science? In this sense, mental health has more the attributes of a religion or a political system.

Returning to Mowrer, we find that he postulated an alternative theory to psychoanalysis. In schematic form, Mowrer argued that good mental health could be achieved only by having the individual live in harmony or concordance with his conscience. That is, the clients had to *assume* that the conscience was immutable and correct and that what we believed, said, and did had to be in agreement with the fundamental tenets of the conscience. Mental illness emerged when the patient, through deceit, violated the dictates of the conscience. Good mental health supposedly developed by staying in congruence with the conscience.

Whether one chooses to accept Mowrer's fundamental reinterpretation of psychoanalysis would seem to be a question of personal preference. However, as part of his overall theoretical approach he made several observations that have influenced the development of our agency. First, he questioned Freud's deterministic orientation. Mowrer felt that the patient had to held responsible for his behavior, i.e., the patient had made decisions that resulted in his current dilemma. In treating patients, Mowrer placed the responsibility on the patient to make new decisions that would extricate him from his personal difficulties.

Second, Mowrer was one of the first to understand that those problems subsumed under mental health and mental illness were of a very extensive nature. He knew that these problems would not be resolved merely by developing new clinical technology. Mowrer felt that Freud and Dewey with their emphasis on expression and permissiveness had disrupted some of our basic social institutions, e.g., the family, the school, and the church. Thus, Mowrer planted the seeds for the concept of "treatment through institutional change." That is, we can effect more treatment by examining, altering, and creating new institutions than by treating through traditional clinical techniques, such as psychotherapy. Later we will present one of Mowrer's new social institutions—integrity groups, or peer groups—as an example of this thinking. Mowrer played a major role in sensitizing our staff to the importance of examining and altering our social institutions.

Szasz, in a series of books and articles (1961, 1971) and in personal communications, provided many concepts that aided us in reconstituting our agency. We will attempt to describe his position in capsule form. Overall we would say he has a direct commonsense approach, and he makes little use of current psychiatric or psychological theory. We should say that he too began his career as a psychoanalyst and went through a period of working out his feelings toward the Freudian model. Currently he maintains an angry antipsychoanalytical posture.

We can best describe his attitudes toward mental illness in political terms or in the frame of reference of the Constitution. He is primarily concerned about persons who have been made patients involuntarily. His discussions are reminiscent of the great legal debates of the Warren Court. That is, he feels that the role of the involuntary patient is generated from several basic Constitutional matters. There is, on one hand, the basic Constitutional guarantee of self-determination and autonomy, i.e., the individual should have the right to pursue his own way of life. On the other hand, there are guarantees that protect the larger society and safeguard the nation. We are in a continuous struggle of balancing freedom and security. When we involuntarily lock up a person in a mental hospital we are dominated by the motive of security. In that case we are theoretically protecting the society from the individual or the individual from himself. Generally the Constitution provides for imprisonment when the individual violates the rights of others. However, in the context of protecting the individual we have produced an extralegal system of placing individuals in mental institutions.

Szasz feels that patients, like other minorities—e.g., women, children, and blacks—are scapegoated out of a societal paternalism. In effect, we are constantly locking up, exiling, and overtreating, supposedly for the sake of the individual and the greater society. Szasz suggests that out of our need to protect mental patients, we have given caregivers extralegal powers, which has really resulted in the violation of the involuntary patient's rights. Some of the implications of Szasz's positions can be seen in the following one-liners:

1. There is no such thing as mental illness in the sense that we should *assume* that strange behavior results from a "disease process."
2. The individual can make any decision pertaining to himself so long as it does not hurt other people.
3. People who violate the law should go to a correctional institution and not a mental hospital.
4. Suicide is a personal decision.
5. Psychoanalysis is a form of religion.
6. Involuntary patients are a persecuted minority.
7. Declaring persons incompetent or mentally ill are expressions of power struggles.

When Szasz first began producing these writings our agency was still locked into the hospital-specialist-disease-cure paternalism. His major book, *The Myth of Mental Illness*, with its emphasis on volition, responsibility, and consequence, hit our agency like a missile: it radicalized some and made others more conservative. However, it will become clear as we describe the alterations in our system that Szasz's writings have been highly influential in our orientation.

The writings of Mowrer and Szasz supported some observations we had made at our own institution. In the middle 1950's, one of the authors of this book, at the request of a psychology intern, undertook the treatment of a patient who was variously diagnosed schizophrenic reaction, hebephrenic type, and schizophrenic reaction, chronic undifferentiated type, which meant he was very "ill." The intern wanted to participate in the process and, at the same time, did not want to feel that he would be wasting the patient's time or injure the patient. We should say that at the time the therapists were very much caught up in the Freudian approach.

We picked out a patient who had been in the institution nine years and now resided on a "back ward." Our hospital, at the time, was organized around a system of extruding patients to progressively worse wards as the residents' competency declined. This patient had reached the bottom of the elevator in this system. We picked him as our candidate for several reasons:

1. Prior to hospitalization, he had shown certain developed resources, such as being a good musician and attending college for several years.
2. He had humorous qualities that appealed to us.
3. Last, he came running into the office while the psychology intern and I were discussing the possibility of finding a patient to treat.

It should be pointed out that initially we had no hope of effectively intervening with this patient. He was a classic example of the alleged process schizophrenic: i.e., he had an opening phase of illness that resembled catatonia, followed by a regression to paranoid patterns, building his own world, and then a subsequent decline in behavior that was labeled hebephrenic, a kind of anarchy. We wanted to help him, but we had little hope. This was the type of patient that was considered to have a grave prognosis.

In terms of our feelings about the case, our other obligations, and our reservations about spending time with the patient, we arranged to see him twice a week, in one-hour sessions, in the office of the senior therapist. Our therapeutic approach was modeled on the various dyadic systems extant at the time: Rogers (1951), Freud, (1920), Adler (1924), et al. The therapists were to be primarily listeners; the patient was to recognize his illness and accept responsibility for his illness; the therapists were to achieve communication with the unconscious systems and modify them. Fortunately, the patient did not understand our approach, nor did he choose to participate in our nonsense. The following weeks were much like broncobusting without benefit of bridle and saddle.

Before discussing the alleged therapeutic process further, we should examine some of the patient's characteristics. He was entirely without inhibitions. He publicly masturbated and passed gas at the slightest provocation. He thought nothing of urinating where he stood or dropping his pants if he was so disposed. He delighted in his delusions and was more than happy to relate them to any available public. His favorite pastime was eating and his favorite fantasy was cannibalism.

He initially attended the therapy sessions without much coaxing, but once in the session, he refused to participate in the therapeutic context set by the therapists. He proved to have the classically described patterns of the schizophrenic patient as depicted by Bleuler (1911), Hanfmann and Kasanin (1942), Shakow (1946), et al. According to the literature, this was an irreversible process and if treatable, would take a decade. The two therapists "hung in" when it seemed wise to terminate. Finally, our consumer became tired of his role as client and refused to come to the sessions. The two therapists, disregarding their past training which indicated that a patient should be well motivated, literally forced the patient to attend the sessions. In the months that followed, there were attempts by the patient to set fire to the therapist's office, there was urinating in inappropriate spots, restraining, pulling, and tugging. The relationship became a structuring, limiting, and restraining procedure.

We should detour and discuss briefly the structuring, limiting, and restraining procedures. This was the heart of the technology. In our original orientation with this patient, our focus was mostly on analyzing, probing, and seeking out his deepest wishes. Instead of this, we informed our client that we would no longer tolerate his bizarre and deviant behavior. He was told that he would have to live within the same societal ground rules as all members of the community, and that we would take all steps necessary to ensure that these ground rules were followed. If our client urinated on the floor, he would be obliged to clean up the mess. When he refused to attend a session he was forced to come. We took the position that it is impossible to be "crazy" if staff took a determined counterstance.

After several effortful months in which therapy was moved out of the office onto the grounds, to the piano, and into various activities, the entire experience reached a "super" blowup. The patient, by all considerations, seemed to become totally "crazy," screaming, running, jumping, and rolling. When this came to an end through "appropriate" limit-setting, the patient appeared to take a total flip-flop; it was definitely a day and night experience. The patient seemed to capitulate and actually apologized for behaving the way he had for the last nine years. Within a brief period after this, he left the hospital. Unfortunately or fortunately, we never followed up on this patient, nor have we ever heard from him again.

Several other psychologists in our agency, taking a cue from our experience, selected long-term regressed patients for treatment. The therapies were organized around encounters, limit-setting, tight structures, tenacity, and willingness to invest considerable energy. We would like to mention one other dramatic case. This patient was a forty-year-old woman who had been in the hospital for ten years. She had all the horrible diagnoses and was considered to have an extremely poor prognosis. During her ten years at the hospital, many professional persons had attempted to treat her with traditional therapies. In fact, two years before, she had been lobotomized (psychosurgery). One of the psychology interns decided to try his hand at treating her in terms of the model described above. He asked the senior therapist who had treated the previously described patient for his opinion. It was the recommendation of the senior therapist that this was not a treatable client and that the intern would have a better chance of success if he selected a patient who had not been lobotomized. Approximately four months later the "prophet" saw this patient driving her automobile about the community. She had been discharged, obtained a position, and purchased an automobile. In all the cases in which we employed these strategies, we were successful in getting the patients back to their prehospital level of operation and returning them to the community.

This type of clinical experience began to say some new things to us. Suddenly the hospital population seemed to have a better prognosis. Perhaps the patient was not so much a victim of destiny as we originally thought. The illness of the patient seemed to be related in a way to the patient's *decision* to give up his "crazy" behavior much as Mowrer and Szasz suggested. It was also clear that the patient integrated without investigating inner happenings or inner causes. Many things were beginning to come together.

The change process was given further momentum by a Menninger (1961) article. The article described the fate of a French mental hospital during World War II. The hospital was located in the path of the German army that had circled the Maginot Line. Most of the patients had been sent home to their relatives, but 153 patients, who were considered too ill to return to their relatives, were to be escorted to safety by the hospital staff. As was syntonic with the times, the Germans moved faster than the French anticipated and the patients were left on their own. That ended the story until the end of World War II when a commission was set up to determine the fate of the patients. Most of the patients were traced, and of these, 37 percent were found to have made appropriate community adjustments. We have a situation of "hopeless" patients placed in an existential crisis. When they were encumbered with responsibility for themselves and forced to make a decision, they far exceeded the expectancies of the caregivers. Major changes occurred in the absence of a formal "therapeutic" intervention.

In this section of the chapter we have been attempting to identify some of the developing tides that prepared us for change. The seeds of change began to sprout in 1961 when we took our first real step toward change.

## RISING FROM THE ASHES: NEW SOCIAL INSTITUTIONS

### MILIEU THERAPY

In 1961, we introduced a patient government program at our agency. The details of this activity are described in a paper by Fisher (1965b). At the time, we labeled this program "milieu therapy" because the primary purpose of the program was to improve the patients' surroundings, or environment. In actuality, the basic thrust of the therapy was to give the patients the opportunity to participate in decision-making and thus to influence their own destiny. We can better understand this system by examining the format.

The residents would hold meetings twice weekly, with patient officers conducting the business of the meetings. The agenda would concern itself with ward community issues—personal problems could not be discussed at the meetings. The residents were given the opportunity to develop solutions to their community problems, in the form of prepared proposals. The staff would meet twice weekly to discuss the residents' proposals. If the ward staff could arrive at a decision independent of higher administration, they would respond to the proposal. If higher administrative decisions were necessary, the proposals would be properly channeled. We always provided feedback at the patient meetings.

The reader can better understand the operation of the group by reading the Cumming and Cumming (1962) work on milieu therapy. The major question in the utilization of this model is raised by Fisher (1965b) in the following quotation:

> Implicit within the milieu therapeutic system is the question whether the psychological systems can be altered with *minimum* intrapsychic intervention (changes in the inner man). It is basic to the milieu therapy model *assumptions* that environmental reorganizations change the role of the patients and influence their basic behavioral patterns. That is, we assume that milieu therapy can reduce symptom patterns, re-establish the prehospitalization personality and possibly bring about major shifts in the makeup of the individual. If so, at least in part, the milieu therapies do what the specific treatment systems claim to do.

We will list below the implications of this quotation and the questions raised by the quotation:

1. Can a person be changed without specific therapeutic treatment?
2. Can effective intervention be entirely in the social systems (environmental) without traditional therapy?
3. Does allowing a patient to participate in his own destiny—i.e., make decisions—prove to be a therapeutic factor?
4. Does increased responsibility have therapeutic impact on the residential patient?
5. Is it possible that new roles and new role expectancies feed back into the patient as change factors?

At the time, we were really in no position to evaluate the effectiveness of the program scientifically. The following quotation by Fisher (1965b) demonstrates the impact of the milieu therapy.

> The ward meetings have spread throughout the hospital. Instead of one program, there are now twenty and some of these have gone much farther than the original ward. There is now a Therapeutic Council, the first real middle management group in the hospital, which is made up of chiefs of departments, some ward representatives, and assistant department chiefs. The Council attempts to deal with problems which are beyond the authority of the local wards; it has encouraged the development of ward programs; and has aided in educating the staff. About one-fifth of the patients in the hospital are active in some facet of milieu therapy.

At the time, although we were attempting to escape the implications of the Medical-Freudian model, we still had to work through some of our feelings. Instead of pointing out that the Freudian model was invalid, we felt the need to rationalize our posture in the context of the Freudian system. This can be seen in the following quotation by Fisher (1965b):

> Another major impact of the milieu therapy model was the shift in emphasis in the Freudian theory. Cumming and Cumming (1962) brought the role of the Executive Ego to the fore. The Executive Ego is the conscious portion of the ego and is that part of the personality that is more responsive to the environment. In basic Freudian theory, it had been the theme to bring about changes in the unconscious (synthetic) portion of the ego. It was assumed that in this territory there were the causal factors and thus this is where we attempt to bring about changes. In shifting the emphasis towards the Executive Ego, we gave more credence to environmental therapies, role playing techniques and sociological therapies.

## THE UNIT SYSTEM

The second major change at our institution grew out of our increasing sensitivity to environmental influences. It was becoming clear that our large centralized facility was not adaptive to treatment programs. Rowitz and Levy (1971), in speaking of centralized facilities, state: "This type of hospital does not usually encourage the development of effective treatment programs, although treatment is attempted on acute cases."

The large centralized hospital is organized according to a pyramidic structure with the superintendent at the top and patients at the bottom. Staff are linked into the system through departments and speak to the clinical director through the department head, who speaks to the superintendent through the clinical director. As long as the hospital goal is warehousing, the centralized system survives, but if you want to provide services, the system malfunctions. The pyramidic system is a gate-keeping and inhibiting system. It exists because the persons in power are attempting to maintain power in "gangland" fashion. The superintendent, the clinical director, and the department heads despite the total failure of the system justified their position on the basis of credentials, knowledge, expertise, etc. It is very much like being in charge of a bankrupt business and claiming authority on the basis of competency. We will list here the paradoxes and the stupidities built into this pyramidic system.

1. The treatment staff cannot directly respond to the patients' deepest requests. If a patient asks to have a grounds pass or a discharge, the staff working with him has to ask the permission of the distant administrator who has never seen the patient. This is supposedly done because the administrator has expertise in mental illness. No one takes the time to evaluate or establish the expertise. Further, the administrator has typically not seen the pa-

tient, and even if he had expertise, he would not be able to use it. The two main motivations for this system are fear and the attempt to retain power by the higher-level administrators.

2. This system minimizes risk-taking. Few patients receive grounds passes, home visits, or discharges. No one is ever punished for omissions. If you do not do something, there are no consequences. Only acts of commission are punished.

3. The patients and the staff not participating in the crucial decision-making process become alienated and develop major depersonalization and apathy patterns.

4. A class and caste system develops around the power to make crucial decisions. Patients make no decisions and superintendents participate in all decisions—the high and the low.

In response to these issues the hospital decentralized into a unit system in 1963. The large hospital was broken down into ten units: some were specialized units, e.g., the Alcoholic Program; others took patients on a random basis—heterogenous distribution of patients. Staff moved out of departments into programs and the tokens of reward were handed over to program directors instead of department heads. We eventually went out of the department business.

Each program subdivided into ward programs—the ward appeared to be the natural unit of operation. The trend was to form a team on each ward and move the clinical decision-making to the ward level. The people who were spending their time with the patients began making the crucial decisions. The staff working directly with the patients had more confidence in their decision-making; risk-taking increased throughout the system. Staff discharged patients that were once considered untreatable. Competition developed between programs in regard to funding, staffing, and reputation. It became easier to establish patterns of responsibility. Now there were people responsible for wards and programs.

To meet the needs of such programs, we required a different kind of profession. The teams that were established were asked to function as generalists: i.e., teams were primarily of a nonspecialist orientation (the typical bowling team) rather than a team of specialists (a baseball team). We needed employees who would be willing to participate in all tasks necessary to treat patients. In the past, our staff was polarized into an "upper class," the professionals, and a "lower class," the nonprofessionals. The professionals had many skills and appropriate sensitivities but chose to work only with the patient's "mind." The nonprofessionals appeared willing to do anything but frequently lacked the sensitivities to deliver services in a therapeutic fashion. As we developed the theme of the generalist a number of issues seemed to be clarified. We decided that in a mental health system which is minimally funded, you do better with generalists who are willing to do anything than with specialists who will do only "their thing." We found that the concept of the generalist resulted in the development of a "middle class." We no longer had the polarized society of professionals versus nonprofessionals. The generalist concept works in well with a career ladder. It becomes theoretically possible that anyone in our system might eventually become "President." It is a potential relinking system for patients and employees. The introduction of this new profession aided in the rethinking of what the crucial ingredients are in our employees. We have come to believe that the personal equation factor is the prime quality in developing an effective caregiver. That is, what a person brings into the situation in regard to energy, appearance, size, and interpersonal skills seems to be more important than education. Of course, this is not to deny that appropriate education and training can add important facets to the appropriate person. With the development of this new profession, we have had more input into their training, and they arrive on the ward better prepared to provide the services we need. Traditional professions are trained and recruited by universities into work patterns that are irrelevant for our type of service operation—possibly any service operation. The concept of the generalist has played a major role in reconstituting our agency.

## THE CATCHMENT MODEL

In 1968 our agency went through a major reorganization in order to improve our effectiveness. At this time we organized around a "catchment" model. That is, we created programs that only served specified geographical areas. At the heart of the catchment concept is the nonextrusion theme. That is, all patients coming to the door of the program serving that area are provided with a meaningful response. The program is responsible for all patients in the geographical area from birth to death regardless of severity of problem. It further becomes the responsibility of the catchment to assure continuity of service. Services occurring in the community have to be related to services occurring in the residential facility, which in turn, have to be related to services occurring after discharge.

## RESULTS AND IMPLICATIONS

We feel that the crucial factor in these themes is in their social implications. We had to deal with everybody, not just those patients we liked or those we considered to have a good prognosis. This meant that programs had to develop broad-spectrum intervention procedures to cope with heterogenous population. It was no longer possible to segregate patients or give up on patients. Those patients who were abandoned would now gather dust in the program's own backyard. This would obviously turn programs around in terms of services and delivery of services.

Institutions falling of their own weight are no longer a

novelty in Western society. Our institution declined because we were unable to respond to the various publics and consumers that we served. For several decades, we continued to serve our consumer groups with therapeutic modalities and delivery systems that were designed for a smaller and different population. We are firmly convinced that organizations must be in a constant process of change to meet the needs and pressures applied by their various consumers and publics. Organizations must remain responsive to these needs or they become stagnant and ineffective.

In this chapter we have described the process by which we attempted to reconstitute ourselves. The seeds for change were planted in the late '50s, the process for change began in the early '60s, and we feel that this change system continues. We did not create a Camelot, but we did manage to bring about some significant alterations.

1. We reduced our patient population from nearly 7,000 to 1,761 (as of June, 1972).
2. We increased our staff from 1,000 to 1,790.
3. We have managed to rid ourselves of our poorest residential facilities.
4. We have influenced the construction of a number of new buildings as well as remodeling some old ones.
5. We formerly served no outpatients. We currently serve 1,500 people in the community.
6. In the past, over 60 percent of the patients entering the hospital were involuntary. As of now, at least, 70 percent are voluntary.

We are suggesting that these changes were a result of our rethinking traditional concepts in mental health and challenging the existing assumptions. In the next two chapters we shall examine the "great issues" in mental health and study their implications for the society as a whole.

# IV

## Great Issues in "Treatment Through Institutional Change": Part I

In Chapters II and III we presented the configuration of "critical mass" in our institution as well as the antidote to "critical mass"—"treatment through institutional change." We attempted to relate these events to treatment models, treatment delivery systems, and organizational models. In Chapters IV and V we will attempt to identify, clarify, and define key issues relevant to the concepts of "critical mass" and "treatment through institutional change."

As part of the mythology that we can distinguish normal from abnormal and healthy from unhealthy, caregivers have identified persons, relationships, and institutions as unhealthy and have interfered in persons' rights and behavior which are probably none of their business. In a recent motion picture, *The Godfather*, Marlon Brando, who plays the head of a Mafia family, a Godfather, moralizes, advises, and provides suggestions for good mental health: e.g., spend a lot of time with your family, trust no one, the first one who suggests a meeting with the opposition is the spy, etc. One cannot help considering the possibility that this is a caricature of the ultimate mental health worker.

Caregivers are caught up in the same mythology as the Godfather—they believe that they know what is best for the client. Operating from this *assumption*, they disrupt their client's living style, gangster-like, frequently without constructive alternatives.

## EXAMPLES OF CAREGIVER OMNIPOTENCE

### ANECDOTE I

This is a situation which occurs rather frequently. A young person enters the hospital after a struggle with his family concerning drugs, responsibility, girl friends, and/or education. The staff may, after due consideration, decide that this is a sick family and side with the youngster. In fact, they may encourage, explicitly or implicitly, rebellion or subversion against the family. The youngster then strikes out more intensely against the family, widening the gap to a point bordering on total alienation. The family breaks communication, stops visiting, and does not write. No one on the staff has a good alternative to the family; therefore we have had a Hungarian rebellion, i.e., there is no way for the client to win. The patient is now in the position that he must stay in the hospital or capitulate to the family. The staff omnipotence has placed the patient in a totally untenable position.

### ANECDOTE II

A social worker accidentally finds out about an incestuous situation and investigates. He discovers that a man in his sixties has been maintaining an incestuous relationship with his thirty-year-old daughter for five years. The mother, father, and daughter have agreed to the relationship. The social worker takes it upon himself to petition for the commitment of father and daughter. As a result the father loses his job and is committed; the daughter loses her job and is committed; the mother, without any means of support, goes on public aid.

Eventually, the family lose their home, and the father and daughter become institutionalized. Staff has spoken!

### ANECDOTE III

A man in therapy is encouraged by the therapist and friends to give up a long-term homosexual relationship with an older man. The older man not only has been a sexual partner but has provided other forms of help: career advice, job advice, occasional financial support, and emergency help on several occasions. The young man seeking the "land of normality" gives up his male friend for a young lady. He does not love her, but in his all-out pursuit of "normality" he marries and begins housekeeping. Within a year he becomes sufficiently disturbed to be labeled schizophrenic by his mental health advisers and is locked up in a state hospital. The young wife quickly abandons him, the old friends are gone, and he becomes a victim of institutionalization. You have to ask, What is this all about?

### RESULTS OF CAREGIVER OMNIPOTENCE

It is our contention that atrocities of a similar nature are practiced in our communities because of the mythologies and "delusions" relating to the Medical-Freudian system. We feel that there exists every combination and permutation of error possible. People who want help are unable to obtain it. People who do not want help have it forced upon them. People are ushered into inappropriate services. The population that probably least needs mental health services has the greatest resources available. Clients requiring only emergency intervention end up being recruited into a mental health network that results in an interminable relationship. The list of atrocities, stupidities, and paradoxes is endless.

In this chapter and the next we will attempt to identify key concepts and issues that result in the confusion, ambiguity, and stupidity in the field. We have touched on some of these factors in the first three chapters, but at this point we will attempt to identify clearly and delineate these concepts and issues.

## THE ISSUES OF OBJECTIVITY, EVALUATION, ECONOMY, AND CAPRICIOUSNESS

The problems in the field probably began with our inability to evaluate our services or develop a meaningful or identifiable economy. This idea can probably better be understood in the light of several analogies. If an individual opens a business in the American economy, we would further evaluate the strategies, tactics, techniques, and equipment of the business with regard to whether they led to increased or decreased profits.

We can employ a second analogy from the field of the physical sciences. The economy in these areas is based on finding the truth through brilliant research, conceptualizations, and theories. Achievement, status, and wealth in scientific endeavors are based on scientific success.

Mental health workers have not totally ignored the issues of evaluation and economy. There have been spasmodic attempts to assess therapy systems and therapists but certainly always without success. We are unable to say with any degree of certainty that any therapy system works. Professionals still argue which is the best treatment system. We have no evidence to prove that one person is a superior therapist to another. The reader can ask the most fundamental question about mental health or treatment and be certain there is no objective, scientifically supported answer. It is this lack of meaningful evaluation which leaves the field in shambles.

We have the situation of endless messiahs laying claim to new therapy techniques that will revolutionize the field. Each of the new movements seems through parthenogenesis to produce prodigal offspring who develop variations on variations. It is reminiscent of the endless mitosis in the French political spectrum prior to DeGaulle. In this sense it is also like pop music. Each school has a short life followed by a new fad, on into infinity.

The deeper problem lies in the power structure. Unlike scientific discipline, where knowledge provides constraints, each new agency director or any governor *can* develop new policies for an agency based purely on his whims. It is not unusual for a new governor to appoint a new department director who will in terms of his personal prejudices attempt to change the course of the department. Those changes may be based on political expediency, a new passing fad, or the prejudices of influential persons. Changes never emerge from new scientifically validated findings. It will help the reader to understand that the physical sciences are not the proper analogues for happenings in the field of mental health. The reader will understand the system much better by utilizing analogues in gamesmanship, religion, and politics.

Mental health workers ignore their lack of scientific validation and function as if they are dealing with the truth. We will present a brief dialogue to make this point.

TRUE BELIEVER THERAPIST: My friend called me and said Mrs. Smith was very depressed, but she didn't know why. In about a half hour they arrived at my office. Mrs. Smith was crying and her friend, Mrs. Jones, was trying to provide moral support.

CYNIC AND SKEPTIC: What did you do? How did you handle it?

TRUE BELIEVER THERAPIST: I asked Mrs. Smith if she wanted Mrs. Jones to stay or leave. Mrs. Smith decided she wanted her friend to be present in the situation. (Having an accompanying friend sit in is not typical.)

CYNIC AND SKEPTIC: How did you feel about the friend sitting in? Why did you ask Mrs. Smith for her opinion? (We don't think it is a bad notion, but we are curious about the approach.)

TRUE BELIEVER THERAPIST: I would rather work with groups, and I think the support of a group is more powerful than the support of one person. (It is a preference and a belief.)

CYNIC AND SKEPTIC: Why do you believe this?

TRUE BELIEVER THERAPIST: It works for me and that is the opinion of experts. (Needless to say, there are a lot of different experts, and no one can define what makes an expert.)

CYNIC AND SKEPTIC: Well, how did you handle the situation?

TRUE BELIEVER THERAPIST: I asked her to tell me what happened. Mrs. Smith tearfully related a story of finding her husband having an affair with his twenty-one-year-old office assistant—Mr. and Mrs. Smith are in their early fifties. The husband became upset and left home. After she related her story, I told her to bring her feelings out where we could look at them. While she cried and talked, I stroked her and told her she was really a good person. I made her say over and over, "I am a good person." (There were additional comments by the therapist regarding self-image, its development in relationship to parents, and comparing the experience with early childhood experience.)

CYNIC AND SKEPTIC: How was it finally resolved?

TRUE BELIEVER THERAPIST: The patient felt better, and her depression seemed to lift. I am going to see the husband tomorrow and discuss the conditions for reconciliation.

CYNIC AND SKEPTIC (*suggesting an alternative approach*): Suppose we *assume* that she has been a lousy wife and a poor sex partner. The husband, finally not able to take it any longer, found an appropriate substitute and broke away from the miserable wife. The wife is depressed because she can no longer regulate the poor husband and is afraid of the loss of cash. The wife felt better, became less depressed, because the alliance with the therapist increased the possibility of recapturing the husband.

We should say the dialogue is true but schematically presented. We are suggesting that the hypothesis of the Cynic and Skeptic can be as appropriate as the concepts of the True Believer. Each therapist pursues a game plan couched and packaged in scientific jargon with equal potential for the truth. We feel it is crucial that mental health consumers understand the subjectivity which dominates the field and have the opportunity to select their own game plan. Equating game plans with truth leads to much of the confusion in the field.

## The Issue of Boundaries

This section is closely related to the above section dealing with evaluation and economics. We are going to force the reader to work in this section, partly because we ourselves do not fully understand the issue and partly because communication in this never-never land is difficult.

In discussing boundaries in mental health, we have to start by saying that they are difficult to identify or delineate. You are forever surrounded by ambiguity and confusing paradoxes. This vagueness exists throughout the system from the most petty issues to the most significant and relevant ones. We will provide examples of this vagueness.

1. A professional worker arrives late for work. There will be endless arguments about how to handle this problem. It is seldom that there will be a clear rule such as docking late workers regardless of status of professions.

2. A man commits a crime. A decision has to be made whether he should go to prison or to a mental hospital. It is absolutely impossible to set guidelines for such a decision. The lack of clear boundaries allows prejudice, pettiness, and political favoritism to intrude and determine the results.

3. The length of treatment appears to be a totally arbitrary matter determined by fads, the consumer's resources, the therapist's needs, and family attitudes.

There are many more such areas of ambiguity and vague boundaries. We realize there are dangers in closing a system by developing too many hard boundaries, but we don't feel that we are approaching such a danger point at present. A good example of the type of boundary to which we are referring is the nonextrusion clause in the catchment system. In this type of system a specifically defined geographic area is designated as a "catchment." When you ask a catchment program director for which patients he has responsibility the answer is clear— everyone living in the boundaries of his territory from birth to death. If things do not go well in a particular geographical area, we know who should be held responsible.

We are suggesting that contingent upon the game plan, a service program should establish boundaries. When a patient enters a treatment system, we should set the day for termination of therapy. If someone commits a crime, we should have an agreed-upon rule as to what agency should handle lawbreakers. This will work better than *assuming* that experts can really make accurate, subjective discriminations. We suspect that it is an error to allow caregivers extralegal powers. The control of inpatients should be determined by the number of beds an agency has. If a state agency has one hundred beds, the agency should be forced to live within that restriction. If the one hundred and first patient enters the agency, someone has to be discharged.

We don't mean that the boundaries cited above have to be accepted, or that once a boundary is established it cannot be altered. However, we feel that more boundaries, constraints, and expectations have to be placed on caregivers. This is for the good of the consumer as well as of the workers. We feel that without a meaningful evaluation or economy the boundaries of the existing game plans should be carefully defined.

## THE ISSUES OF INFORMATION, OPTIONS, AND GAME PLANS

The lack of appropriate evaluation, the inability to establish a meaningful economy, the inability of caregivers to bring mental health issues under the laws of science, and the failure to define boundaries leave the consumer in a vulnerable position. "How do I solve my problems? Whom should I select as a therapist? How do I know that I am getting my money's worth? How long will therapy last?" The patient has to make important decisions without objective answers or adequate information. This situation parallels in many ways such questions as: "What religious preference is most likely to get me into heaven?" "What political system is most likely to lead to utopia?" Instead of providing absolute answers to these complex questions at this point, we will glance at three broad approaches to mental health problems. In Chapters VI, VII, and VIII we will more carefully develop the options.

### APPROACHES TO MENTAL HEALTH PROBLEMS

### Medical-Freudian Model

We have discussed this approach in some detail in earlier chapters; here we will just note several key points. The Medical-Freudian approach focuses on the individual and *assumes* that proper treatment demands internal change. It is certainly the most commonly identified treatment model. Finally, this model focuses primarily on sophisticated clinical techniques. There is a technology orientation among clinicians that obscures all other treatment forces. That is, persons trained in the clinical mold *assume* that techniques such as nondirective therapy, interpretation, dream analysis, psychodrama, etc., are the antidotes to human problems.

## Public Health Model

This model, in part, is an outgrowth of the medical public health model but has taken on unique characteristics that make it substantially different. Caplan (1964) is the seminal leader of this movement.

In the long run, the public health model is preventative in nature. We can begin to understand this model by an example. An expert in the field might be interested in the impact of death within the primary family unit. In order to study a facet of this problem, investigators might study families in which the father dies suddenly and unexpectedly. It might be a long-term study of the impact of a father's death on different family styles, family attitudes toward death, age, number of dependents, etc. The study might result in recommendations to families regarding death, important losses, and separations. The recommendations might have implications for education, counseling, mourning, and the type of resources necessary to cope with such experiences. The emphasis is not so much on treatment after the fact as it is on education and intervention that will provide a preventative approach to the problem.

Psychiatrists, psychologists, social workers, and other caregivers are massively ignorant of the impact of cultural experiences, social institutions, institutional change, and various cultural traumas on the developing child, the person in crisis, and the declining geriatric client. We have only the vaguest knowledge of what kinds of experiences are necessary to provide the individual with growth experiences. It is this type of knowledge vacuum that has resulted in our retaining failing school systems long after they have become ineffective, or allowed mental health workers, in the past, to retain large numbers of persons in state hospitals for years despite the destructive impact of these institutions.

If we are able to understand the impact of social institutions on behavior and changing behavior, our capacity to help large numbers of persons would be vastly increased. In the state hospitals it has been *assumed* that patients who are held much beyond ninety days become institutionalized. This means that we not only have to deal with the difficulties which brought the person to the institution but in addition we have to deal with problems created by the institutionalization. Longer stays mean decreased motivation to return to former life-styles. The patient's social network reorganizes without him if he is not discharged in a reasonable period of time. This information results in state hospitals maximizing early discharges, maximizing a patient's contact with his social network, and organizing their treatment programs toward discharge. This has been an important factor in reducing patient loads in hospitals (an example of "treatment through institutional change").

There are probably many analogies to this state hospital situation in community situations. It is quite possible, certainly worth considering, that individual therapy contacts beyond a certain length of time result in a dependency relationship between patient and therapist that is difficult to terminate. The therapist in effect has promised a nonexistent "rose garden." It becomes an add-on problem to the problems that the patient originally brought to therapy.

Many community clinics maintain long waiting lists for their patients because of staff shortages. In fact, we recently heard of a clinic that had an eight- or nine-month waiting list for neurological evaluations (an example of a "critical mass" situation). The painful part of this business is the casual attitude of the clinics, and the community's acceptance of such atrocities. These clinics operate in the Medical-Freudian model: see patients with the best prognosis, see patients on a one-to-one basis, maintain long-term therapy relationships, allow staff members to funnel the better-paying clients into their private practice. Although most patients coming to clinics or needing clinical services do not require medical services, the greatest portion of the clinic budgets goes into paying psychiatrists (for these community services psychiatrists receive about twenty dollars an hour) who out of the goodness of their hearts give one day a week. We know of one service clinic with long waiting lists that allowed two of its part-time psychiatrists to participate in irrelevant personal research. It is worth considering how many patients on *waiting lists* die, commit suicide, become fixed in maladaptive behavior, or commit crimes.

Despite the great potential of this public health approach, few resources are available for this model. Little attention is given at caregivers' conventions to public health issues. Most funding goes to the treaters and clinical technologists attempting to find the mental health Rosetta stone.

## Human Service Model

We can start this section by asking, Why do patients come to the doors of caregivers? If one asks the client, he may say, "I am sick." The patient gives this as his reason, because he feels that this is the basic justification for seeking out a therapist. Further questioning will typically demonstrate concrete and realistic needs for help: loss of job, family fight, caught in an indiscretion, being overwhelmingly in debt, etc. We will present two brief dialogues to demonstrate this point of view.

*Situation I—Private Practice Situation.* The patient has called for an immediate appointment. She sounds desperate and seemingly in need of immediate help. We will omit the initial amenities.

PROBLEM SOLVER: (We will use this title rather than therapist with its obvious implications.) You seem very upset. Can you tell me what is distressing you?

CLIENT: I am confused and frightened. I am depressed, and I feel like committing suicide. My situation seems hopeless.

PROBLEM SOLVER: Are you able to tell me what has caused this distress?

CLIENT: I know, but I am ashamed. It is hard to talk about it.

PROBLEM SOLVER: It helps to talk about it. When you get the situation out into the open it seems to reduce the pain.

CLIENT: Well, I guess that is why I came here. For the first time since I have been married I had an affair. I am very ashamed.

PROBLEM SOLVER: (The problem solver is under the *assumption* that this is a recent event.) When did it occur?

CLIENT: It began about six months ago at the place where I worked. I began an affair with a customer.

PROBLEM SOLVER: Why has it suddenly become so disturbing and urgent?

CLIENT: His wife recently caught us, and she is now threatening to tell my husband. If he finds out, I don't know what he will do.

There is no question that this woman has a real problem, but we are not dealing with a "disease." She has been caught in an embarrassing situation that could lead to a public disclosure, divorce, loss of children, and a general disruption of her way of life. There is no "cure" or "medicine" for this problem. The client in this case has to face up to the situation rather than take the posture of a helpless patient waiting to be "cured" of a "disease" for which she has no responsibility. The two participants, the client and the problem solver, must develop a *game plan* for this situation that includes immediate plans and contingency plans depending upon the developing situation. (We would classify this as a problem-solving task.)

In this case, the woman was truly sorry for what she had done and certainly wanted to remain in the marriage. It was her fear of losing her husband that stopped her from confessing and attempting to make reparations. Before she could make a decision about confessing, the other man's wife reported the incident to the client's husband. The husband, of course, became upset and angry—a natural and not a "diseased" reaction. There followed a series of meetings: husband and problem solver, wife and problem solver, husband and wife and problem solver. These sessions focused on analyses of situations, options, and possible consequences. After examining the situation, they decided that maintaining the marriage was the best solution. Several years later the couple were still together. The children had not been significantly disturbed, and neither mate had developed maladaptive behavioral patterns.

*Situation II—State Hospital Situation.* This young man had been brought into the state hospital in a highly agitated state. In the initial evaluation at the time of hospitalization he was said to be confused, hallucinating, and behaving like an acute schizophrenic.

PROBLEM SOLVER: What brought you into the hospital? (Although we think it absurd to refer to most mental health agencies as hospitals, our clients carry this stereotype and we don't want to involve ourselves in semantic issues.)

CLIENT: I went "crazy"—I began hearing voices. I needed some kind of help.

PROBLEM SOLVER: You felt sick and wanted someone to help you.

CLIENT: Yes, that is it. Things got out of hand. I hope you can fix me up.

PROBLEM SOLVER: Is there anything you can do for yourself?

CLIENT: I tried, but what can you do when you are sick?

PROBLEM SOLVER: Can you tell me how you got into your present situation?

The client related in some detail the events of the last three years; he was twenty-one at the time of the interview. He was forced to get married at eighteen because he impregnated a sixteen-year-old girl. This had ruined his plans to go to college and become a lawyer. He did make an effort to adapt to the situation but he never developed the earning power to meet the demands of his young wife. He piled up debts, avoided bill collectors, lost jobs, and felt as if his life was going down the drain (a problem-solving failure). His values did not allow him to abandon his family and run. He had too much pride to allow his parents to help, and he never became physically ill as he wished. The behavioral pattern described in his medical case folder as schizophrenia was his option to escape an unbearable situation. His problems were not related to "disease." He had lost his dreams. He was not able to find an adaptive job because of age, color, and lack of education. He was unable to run because of a sense of decency. This man had no "disease." Rather, he needed help with money, career, education, and his relationship with his wife.

There are numerous persons who, having become trapped by life's circumstances, simulate a hypothetical disease state in order to escape from an extremely painful situation. In fact, most clients in state hospitals remain or are retained because of resource problems rather than "disease" problems.

Persons who want divorces frequently expedite this process by coming to problem solvers. It would be atypical for someone to arrive at the door of a caregiver seeking help for a divorce. They come for a variety of reasons: wife-beating, jealousy of their mate, marriage counseling, unhappiness, etc. The client, because of his personal "hang-ups," is not able to go directly to a lawyer but goes to the therapist hoping to get his support for divorce. We don't mean this as a *conspiratorial process* but rather as a self-deception process. In fact, many persons have good, realistic reasons but require that extra support to carry out their deep wish. They come to a therapist as a "sick person" and leave free of their troubles.

The types of persons described above are labeled as "sick" when seen by caregivers. If they are to be considered as having a good prognosis, a therapist will insist that they accept the concept of being a "sick" person. When a patient is brought to a state hospital, he is considered as having insight if he answers the question, "Why are you here?" with the statement, "I am sick." This theme is expressed in mental hospitals by the fact that they are accredited by the same process as general hospitals. Everyone who comes to the door of a mental hospital, regardless of his problem, is processed through physical examination and laboratory work-up, is diagnosed, medicated, and made to feel "sick."

In an article on lay analysis, Freud (1964) indicated that most patients who seek mental health services do not require medical help. In fact, there are many administrators, medical and nonmedical, who will admit in private conversation that most clients who enter state hospitals require human services and not medical services. The process of accrediting mental hospitals and utilizing the medical model is more politically and public relations oriented than service oriented. Publics still prefer to see human adjustment problems as medical rather than as adjustment and problem-solving tasks.

## A Human Service Model for State Hospitals

In terms of our present thinking we would divide a state hospital into three sections: a small section would be in the Medical-Freudian orientation, a second section would be a voluntary Human Services Section, and the third section would be an Involuntary Security Section.

### Medical-Freudian Section

This section would deal with persons who have physical disorders that are clearly causing behavioral reactions. This might include persons who are having toxic reactions after alcoholic and drug intoxication. It is also probable that metabolic disturbances might cause bizarre behavior. This section would include a small portion of the hospital.

### Human Services Section (voluntary)

This would be a communitylike operation for people who cannot function in traditional towns, villages, and cities. The person would have responsibilities in regard to self and community. The help provided would include problem-solving, finances, relinking to the outside community, survival training, occupations, etc. There would be no requirements in regard to length of stay.

### Involuntary Security Section

This section would be for persons who do not want to come but whose behavior violates the rights of others. We would distinguish them from prisoners because we would *assume* that their behavior resulted from intense emotional reactions which interfered with or interrupted their volitional behavior. We are ambivalent about this solution. In the long run we feel that Szasz's solution, which places all lawbreakers in prisons, is a more even-handed Constitutional solution.

This trisectioned model would save a great deal of money and manpower. It would eliminate many routine medical services that are unnecessary for many persons seeking sanctuary in a state hospital. It would allow many of the clients to participate actively in the helping system, thus reducing the number of employees. It would provide individuals with the opportunity of looking for help without taking on the pattern of *sickness*. This suggested trisectioned approach would be an example of "treatment through institutional change."

# V

## Great Issues in "Treatment Through Institutional Change": Part II

While writing this book, we have found many eventful things occurring around us that we feel should be included. At times, because of recurrent crises, it seems the book should be a diary. We recently had several contacts, one "semitraumatic" and the other two friendly and thoughtful. These events are related to the chapters on "great issues," and we feel that although portions of this material may be slightly redundant, there is enough current drama around the issues to make them worth examining.

### CONFLICT BETWEEN TRADITIONAL AND NEW CONCEPTS OF MENTAL HEALTH CARE

As we were about to begin working on this chapter, a State Legislative Visitation Committee returned for a third visit to our agency. As a little background to their visitation, we should make it clear that the first author of the book was certainly one of the primary persons being scrutinized, examined, and/or investigated by this committee. In this sense the committee's actions led to considerable soul-searching by the author.

At this point, for the next few pages, in order to prepare the way for understanding some emotionally laden issues, we will detour from the format of the book. This will not be a "we section," but an "I section" by Walter Fisher—it will be some personal recollections, introspections, and affects.

I should say that when the Legislative Committee initially came to our agency I had no particular anxieties about the experience, probably because I had no personal experience with such groups. In my own nonhumble way, I thought of myself as one of the "good guys" who had helped to create, plan, support, and fight for most of the constructive happenings in the facility described in Chapter III. However, it does seem that the legislators came to the agency with their eye on me; e.g., they visited only the wards for which I had responsibility and they kept hinting that there was an "evil" person who was intimidating staff. I was later identified as this alleged person.

My first reactions were, of course, extremely defensive. I challenged them to find one person whom I had ever intimidated, and, of course, no such person appeared on the scene. It does turn out, as one always reads, that allegations are printed and refutations are ignored. People who are unhappy write legislators, whereas the satisfied, happy ones never make themselves heard.

After my initial pain subsided, I began to analyze the situation to see if I could understand what happened. To begin with, I accepted the fact that the legislators' viewpoint is much closer to that of mainstream America than my own. It also seemed clear that I was identified as one of the main change agents in the facility and that anyone who felt injured by the changes in the agency probably identified me as one of their primary villains. People don't examine a person's motivation for change. Observations are based primarily on happenings and subsequent consequences to the individual.

The primary treatment model at our agency since the early '60s may be called "treatment through institutional change." Obviously, every time we reorganized to increase the effectiveness of our organization, someone was personally hurt or felt hurt. Even in industry where reorganizations can be justified on the basis of increased profits, such reorganizations meet with great pain. In our subjective system it is difficult to prove that the new game plan is superior, particularly to the person who feels that he has been injured by the changes. We had the additional problem of developing new systems that were incongruent with traditional models of treatment and social expectancies. When the dust began to settle, the primary criticisms of the legislators were as follows:

1. Our facility was not as clean as they would like.
2. We should move away from the generalist model and employ housekeepers, dietary workers, and other support staff.
3. We should increase our security staff and security in general.
4. We should segregate the sexes, in that they should not live in the same wards.
5. We should alter our current high discharge rate and accept the fact that there are some patients who will never be able to be discharged.

I realized that this was at least in part the voice of the people. This was certainly the classical encounter of voices from the past and the forces for reconstituting the system. In agencies with limited resources, operations are based on priorities. The legislators, and possibly the public, want us to work from models such as the Medical-Freudian model and its corollary system, security and cleanliness. We, however, feel that our thrust is to minimize institutionalization, which means a great focus on discharge. (We have been spelling out this orientation throughout the book.)

Administrators in the Department of Mental Health are seriously considering altering portions of the department's model because of pressures placed on them by the legislators. I am not personally critical of them because of this. It is true that, like all human beings, they have personal security needs, but I feel that other issues are involved. Have mental health workers moved too far away from the position of their consumers and attentive publics? How do we bring our constituent lay groups on board? In fact, I found that a number of persons working for me on the wards whom I considered progressive suddenly petitioned me to move away from the generalist approach. These staff persons, who considered themselves professionals, no longer wanted to be involved in the everyday milieu of their patients. They wanted to return to the role of specialist, working only with the patient's "mind" and leaving the rest of the patient's systems to the lower echelons—the psychiatric aides. (In our system, aides are called technicians.)

In the dynamics described in the "I section" by Fisher, we can further identify and clarify some of the "great issues." Identification and clarification begin with the question, What does the consumer want?

### TRADITIONAL VIEW OF MENTAL HEALTH CARE

In the above question, we are, of course, talking of the mainstream consumer. A student in a clinical psychology class at Roosevelt University, somewhat critical of the approach of this book, characterized the consumer position rather well. We will paraphrase the position: "You people are taking away our cherished beliefs. We have been brought up to believe that there are experts in mental health who are available if we become ill. These are persons cast in the medical mold who have the technology to cure us of our diseases. You are telling us that this is possibly or probably not true, or at least you are saying there is no evidence to support this position. This means that if we need help, there is no place to go. We feel that you are taking things apart, but you are not putting new things in their place."

We will paraphrase the response to the student: "It is true that we are not providing you with the type of answer that you want. It is true that in the Medical-Freudian approach the therapists act as if they have a ready-made prescription for your problems, and I suppose that has comforting qualities. The fact that these 'patent medicines' have not worked, and that the model provides little for most people does not seem to disturb the greater percentage of consumers. It seems horrendous that a sterile system continues to survive because people want their opiates. The Freudian system, the Jungian system, the Adlerian system, etc., were life-styles developed by these men. They were systems these men developed for problem-solving their lives. Certainly anyone who wants to mimic the life-styles of Freud, Jung, or Adler has the right to make that choice but to assume that these approaches are panaceas that everyone must accept is an absurdity."

Freud, Jung, Adler, *et al.*, set personal examples for each of us. They made serious attempts to define operationally their life-styles for public consumption. It would probably be useful for each individual to develop a problem-solving style for coping with life problems and stresses. Indeed, we all do develop problem-solving styles. If each of us sat down and described our careers, values, morals, beliefs, etc., and presented these as models for dealing with mental problems, we would in a gross way be mimicking Freud.

This comparing of life-styles to Freudian theory probably pains the majority of caregivers. Most publics and consumers want to believe there is a true way to achieve mental health. Despite the lack of evidence, and because of the consumers' needs, they want to believe that the therapist, through his educational process, really understands the road to mental health. The facts are that most university professors in the caregiving professions have spent little time treating or serving persons who are designated as mentally ill. The mental health knowledge that the caregivers have attained seems to do nothing for themselves or their families in achieving constructive adaptations; witness the high suicide and divorce rates among these same caregivers. There has never been a study to support the hypothesis that caregivers or their families have attained superior adjustments.

In reality, the experience designated as therapy is a risk-taking process—a fact that the patient finds difficult to accept. In this relationship, the client is asked to give up "a bird in the hand for two in the bush," but there are no guarantees. The entire process is unpredictable. There are all the risks extant in any change process: a revolution starts and no one knows where it will end; the American civil rights movement has an autonomy of its own without a predictable outcome. It is this uncertainty about the future which creates the need in the consumer for an "elite" therapist with an alleged surefire treatment model.

The consumer operating out of the God model invests his faith in the therapist rather than insisting on a meaningful evaluation of the alleged treatment systems. A person attending the "proper" school for a long period of time is assumed to be an expert in caregiving. We believe in therapists, grant them extralegal powers, and accept their opinions and prejudices as valid facts. These are acts of faith. The caregivers accept this faith with the same modesty as any god.

Although it is acceptable to laugh at psychiatrists or ridicule psychoanalytical jargon, an attack on the caregiving aspects of the systems approaches violating a societal taboo.

### TRADITIONAL ROLE OF THE CONSUMER

In the system as it exists (the Medical-Freudian model), we have the expert (defined by the school system) who is going to deliver the "medicine" that will "cure" and the consumer or patient who will be "cured" if he will take his "medicine." Throughout this relationship the therapist is the expert, the protector, the teacher, and the leader. The patient is obviously seen as someone lower (different class or caste), passive, in need of protection (paternalism). Frequently the therapist approaches the patient like an old protective "auntie" or the "chicken soup" mother who will tend to her charge until he has achieved the appropriate maturity—the "cure." The field often attracts mothering types, homosexuals working out their identities with their mothers and aunts, and "good-hearted" do-gooders providing "libido baths" and what they describe as quality treatment—an endless relationship.

Many of the criticisms made against the author at our institution relate to the fact that we expect our agency residents to behave like people rather than patients. We do not see the residents as sick persons needing mother's care. We expect our residents to participate with the staff in maintaining their wards, themselves, and the general ecology. Those persons living and working on the ward should develop a contract among themselves as to the functioning of the program. Traditionalists might say that we should take care of these "poor devils" and make sure they receive the proper care—this is clearly the attitude of the Legislative Visitation Committee.

We feel that the milieu in which the individual lives often undoes the value of any specific therapeutic transaction. Treatment systems often recruit persons into new ways of life in which they do not have the resources to function—it is often like the old saying, "How you gonna keep 'em down on the farm, after they've seen Paris?" The recruitment impact of the Medical-Freudian pattern is tremendous. It provides an end-run experience in which the patient finds a relationship with a person that would never have occurred in any of life's ordinary interpersonal transactions. The therapist as the hero destroys the patient's past dreams without providing new ones comparable to his current, unreal relationship with the therapist. The patient, quite logically, retains his relationship with the therapist as long as possible—the interminable therapy.

The consumer is led to believe by traditional therapy systems that his problems are only in himself, and that he can be "cured" and achieve utopia in his role as patient and in his transactions with his therapist, "The Doctor." He must place himself in the hands of his "Doctor" and all will be well. We are suggesting that most services provided to a person identified as emotionally disturbed, "crazy," or mentally ill should not be identified with institutionalized or ritualistic therapy models. It is probably true that there are times when a person feels he is in crisis and feels he should turn to an "expert" for "first aid." However, the broader problems of mental health are society-wide and the responsibility of all citizens. Each time a citizen votes, with the passage of every law, and with each ruling of the Supreme Court, there is an impact on the adaptation patterns of all citizens. Every new piece of civil rights legislation reverberates throughout the society. Consumer protection laws influence our immediate living experiences and make our days more or less stressful. It is not our suggestion that every decision should be made on the basis of creating more or less anxiety, but we should be sensitized to the impact of environmental patterns on our psychological makeup. We cannot allow our society to deteriorate and hope to resolve our problems in the "back room" of the "therapist's shop." Such solutions are too much like retiring to an opium den.

## NEW CONCEPTS: COMMUNITY MENTAL HEALTH SYSTEMS

The development of community mental health systems are first attempts in involving the society in the mental health movement. We should say that in a theoretical sense we support the movement, but there are practical problems that must be resolved before we can make our personal commitment in this direction.

We should first describe and delineate characteristics of this movement. Primarily, it is an attempt to alter the power base in the field of mental health. Currently, the Federal Government and the state governments are the primary resources for delivering mental health services. They provide most of the money, employ most of the caregivers, and serve the greatest number of clients. These government agencies provide these services directly and also provide support for other groups (county government, city government, and nonprofit private organizations) by means of grants. Throughout this book we have pointed out the many evils related to large government bureaucracies' managing and regulating human service agencies. We would think that by now the reader understands our opposition to this system.

The community mental health movement is one of the developing "antidotes" to the large bureaucracy. However, there are some major problems relating to this approach that should be examined. In effect, this movement is an attempt to transfer the power base from large government units to the people. What this generally means is that cities or counties become the new governmental power base, and in addition, we have both citizens' advisory boards and universities pursuing power. These groups would gain control over funding, employment, and the nature of the services to be delivered.

This transfer of power has the appearance of a positive development, but there are a number of observations that should be made. California has developed a system of transferring the mental health power base from state to county government. The reports on this transfer seem to indicate that in some cases this has improved services, and in other situations it has resulted in a decline in services. Traditionally, county governments are more conservative, less well monitored, and provide poorer services than a large governmental unit. County jails are typically the worst jails in the state. Although state prisons are poor, they are like hotels compared to these county jails. In states where public aid is in the hands of counties, there will be a few counties that provide good services, but in general, this is not the case. It is traditionally true that in terms of governmental units we more frequently see the tyranny of the majority over the minority in the smaller units of government.

We feel that if we are to move to a transfer of power from large governmental units to smaller governmental units, there will have to be some demonstrated monitoring and evaluation system that guarantees service. We personally doubt the feasibility of such an evaluation system. It is possible that a massive educational approach might prepare smaller governmental units to assume the responsibility for mental health services, but we feel that this is improbable. The fact of the matter is that large government units have always been more concerned, more involved, and more willing to provide services for the disadvantaged.

Our position would be that if we are to move toward the community mental health movement, it would only be at some future time when education and evaluation provide some meaningful guarantees. Probably the current pressure toward community mental health represents a primary interest in power and boondoggling. The county representatives have less interest in the disadvantaged than does the state, but neither the county nor the state has the appropriate attitudes or feelings. "A plague on both their houses." Probably all outside control can be looked upon with suspicion. Probably all searches for power and control have to be questioned. In the next section on resources, we will look at alternatives.

## DEVELOPING TREATMENT MODELS
### CONGRUENT WITH AVAILABLE RESOURCES

Most mental health experts agree that we have probably reached the high-tide point in the expenditure of funds—particularly governmental funds—in the field of mental health. If we accept this prediction (and we have no idea whether it is a valid prediction), the field is indeed in trouble. By no stretch of the imagination have we brought behavioral problems or so-called mental illness under control. There are some who would say that the reduced body count as far as residential patients are concerned indicates a turn in the struggle, but this is clearly a bogus argument. We do feel that the redefinition of who requires residential care has been a meaningful sociological alteration. As a corollary to the concept that most emotionally disturbed persons do not require residential treatment, it is probably true that most persons who do require residential care require it for shorter periods of time—probably less than forty days. These changes of attitudes have reduced the number of inpatients but have in no way reduced the number of individuals having emotional and adaptation problems. The society has an endless number of potential clients who are alienated and sealed off from their own mainstream and require relinking and human service help. The potential consumers for mental health services are endless.

If we continue to provide those services in terms of the current delivery systems—hospitals, private practice, and clinics—there will be no way to meet the enormous needs extant in the society. Despite this ever-increasing crisis, caregivers, for the most part, function in their traditional styles, the universities continue to prepare caregivers in traditional models, and money is still pouring into the same "ratholes." There are endless questions that we must consider in regard to the issue of resources.

1. Who should have the responsibility for delivering mental health resources?
2. Who should have the responsibility for financing mental health services?
3. Should we distinguish between those persons requiring mental health services in a hospital and those requiring mental health services in a human service system?

4. Should we utilize therapy models that require one-to-one relationships over a long period of time when our resources are limited?
5. What are the relationships between mental health, public aid, corrections, and public health?
6. How can universities relink to the delivery of human services?
7. How do we relink the community into participation in the mental health consortium?
8. What is the proper organizational model for mental health delivery systems?

It is imperative that the caregiver develop a treatment model congruent with his resources. In the past, the clinical worker has worked in the rarefied atmosphere of his therapy model and therapy delivery system without consideration for his budget. We have seen clinicians standing knee-high in "snake pits" delivering their concept of "quality care" to one patient while six thousand slowly sank into the limbo of back wards.

Those who argue for a change in the power base suggest that funding used in state government facilities should go into the hands of various local government groups (city and county) and that they will get more for the dollar and provide better services. As we indicated above, we doubt the validity of this argument and there seem to be no substantial data to prove it. Although there are great potential educational factors in the community being held responsible for its own, too often this has led to scapegoating, persecution, and incredible intolerance. Local minority persons in rural communities will quickly tell you that they see the state as a protector against local bigots who would just as soon put them in a local "concentration camp" with the aid of local mental health bigots.

At this point in history, we do not feel prepared to support the motion shifting the power base to local groups. We believe that significant changes can occur only as we move control into the hands of the consumer. Each person must have the right and the opportunity to seek help with a minimum emphasis on external control. We suggest four resource models based on four different types of mental health consumers.

### TREATMENT MODELS BASED ON TYPES OF CONSUMERS

#### I. *Voluntary High-Resource Persons*

Those persons who want help and have their own resources are, of course, totally free to do anything they want. They, obviously, have a right to pursue any type of mental health care that is available, including tea-leaf reading.

#### II. *Voluntary Low-Resource Persons*

We feel it is the right of these persons to pursue those help forms which are available. The control should be in their hands (the clients') either through national insurance and/or available vouchering through state or local government groups. Voluntary persons seeking help should operate in a free and competitive market.

#### III. *Involuntary Persons: High and Low Resources*

These are persons who have in some way violated the law. We would prefer to see all such persons enter the same system rather than have alleged experts attempt to discriminate on the basis of the individual's capacity to determine his own behavior. We consider it a more dangerous practice to give caregivers extra-Constitutional powers than to send all law violators into one system. We are in no way suggesting that all persons entering the system be managed in the same way. If such a system is seen as rehabilitative in nature and not as a punishment system, this concept becomes more acceptable.

IV. *Involuntary Persons: Low Resouces, Who Have Become Incompetent as a Result of Aging, Disease, or External Trauma*

These are persons who require nursing home and hospital care. They should be supported by national insurance and/or a vouchering system supported by a branch of government. This is a right of the citizens and not a privilege. This service should be available in an open and free market.

In effect, we are suggesting new treatment models, new delivery systems, and redefinition of departmental goals and target populations. Certainly, departments such as mental health, corrections, public health, and public aid must consider their relationships to each other and their various consumer groups.

DEPLOYING RESOURCES ON THE BASIS
OF EXPECTED CHANGES IN THE CLIENT

How resources are deployed is contingent upon what we can do for our clients. It has been assumed by most traditional therapy models, such as psychoanalysis, that their intervention model can alter major facets of the individual: traits, character, values, motivation, interests, etc. They assume and predict that the individual emerging from therapy should be a very different organism from the one entering. It is also assumed that such total changes are necessary if the individual is to be considered "cured." The concept of "cure" in mental health has been different from other health "cures." In the traditional somatic illness, the healer is expected to eradicate the disease, but he isn't expected to redo the entire physical system.

As we have indicated in earlier portions of the book, there is no evidence to support the belief that we can bring about major changes in the psychological makeup of the individual. Even if the individual does appear to have gone through major changes after protracted psychoanalysis, we cannot be sure whether the changes are attributable to psychoanalysis, normal maturation, aging, or unknown intervening variables. We have not found a study that attempts to tease out these factors from treatment—particularly in reference to long-term therapy. In most human service functions, it is difficult to find examples of groups who have the power of evaluating the effectiveness of their services. We have asked many university administrators whether they have studies to demonstrate that persons who have obtained college degrees have become more educated than persons of equal intelligence who have not gone to college. No one has been able to point to studies of this elementary type. The omission of such studies has made us question the openness of all human service agencies.

### "First Aid" Therapy

Because there is no support for the belief that we can bring about major changes in the individual, a new attitude has been emerging. This new attitude might be characterized in several ways: symptom removal, behavior change, or "first aid." This approach focuses on removing the problem or difficulty that brought the client into contact with the caregiver. An example of this can be seen in the approach of some state hospitals. A patient is brought into a state hospital because he is suicidal. The staff retain the patient only as long as they consider him suicidal. The patient would not be retained to identify a cause or to bring about some ultimate "cure."

There are some clustering patterns in these expectancies. If you assume that major alterations can be brought about in the basic personality of the individual, you typically retain the person in therapy for a long period of time and maintain expectancies of great change. On the other hand, if you assume that great changes are not possible, you become parsimonious, pragmatic, and develop brief therapy models.

This is obviously a crucial issue in regard to the deployment of resources. It would seem that there should be a national effort to study possible changes that can be brought about in various service models. It is all but impossible to decide on effective expenditures if we don't know what changes are possible or probable. Until it is demonstrated that we can make major therapeutic changes, it would seem inappropriate to offer models that are of long duration in the hope of great changes.

## DESTROYING THE MYTH OF "MENTAL ILLNESS"

Szasz (1961, 1971) has raised serious questions about the concept of mental illness. He recently visited our agency, and it would be fair to say that his objection to the validity of the concept of mental illness is more intense than ever. He suggests that mental illness is really a myth which has emerged out of the analogue that compares maladaptation with physical illness. When you ask professionals, consumers, and attentive publics about their concept of mental illness, the response is typically jargon which when decoded relates to cultural norms, maladaptation in regard to survival, or certain unacceptable forms of behavior. To say that someone is mentally ill or not mentally ill provides absolutely no information. Instead of this broad abstract question, we have to raise a series of operational-type questions:

1. Does this person need to be locked up?
2. Should this person be declared legally incompetent?
3. Should this person go to prison?
4. Does this person require individual counseling?
5. Does this person need to be helped in regard to the cash economy?

Caregivers are continuously forced to answer questions similar to these listed above. There is no question more abstract, more spurious, or more irrelevant than, "Am I mentally ill?" Caregivers are continuously stuttering pompous, meaningless answers to this scholastic type of question. There is perhaps no more absurd scene in the world than a mental health worker sitting behind a desk, pensively puffing his pipe, and pouring out learned answers to his client: "You are sick." "You are neurotic." "You are too sick to be in jail." Unfortunately, too frequently, these "wise" observations have been taken for gospel and individuals' destinies have been determined by this profound arrogance.

Most diagnostic systems have been organized around the concept of type of sickness. It is assumed that the type of sickness correlates with prognosis, length of stay, and kind of treatment. As we reported earlier, Hollingshead and Redlich (1969) have pointed out that in mental health, diagnoses have no relationship to the services and treatment received or provided but are more related to socioeconomic status and color. In general, like most social systems, the traditional diagnostic model has been utilized to support the superiority of the middle class over the lower classes and the white society over the black society.

If we are to develop an appropriate classification model, it must be meaningful in regard to the decision-making process of the caregiver. The main task of caregivers is decision-making and there is little information to aid them in this process. When we say that a person is schizophrenic, it is a totally meaningless message. It tells us nothing of cause, duration of maladaptation, treatment modality, or types of services required. When a person is diagnosed schizophrenic, he may have to be hospitalized or he may not need help; he may maintain the behavioral patterns for a day or for a lifetime; he may be given a lobotomy or he may receive no treatment; he may be a socioeconomic success or he may live in a ghetto.

The question of whether a person is sick should be replaced with the question, Does this person need help? If the person needs help, what kind of help does he need? How can we organize our system to meet the help needs of the consumer?

The search for mental illness, the causes of mental illness, and the treatment of mental illness have led us down a confused and counterproductive pathway.

## REDEFINING THE NATURE OF CAREGIVING

As we reconsider the problems in the field and the "great issues" in mental health, it becomes important to assess the nature of the caregivers. There have been struggles from the beginning as to whom this "turf" belongs to. At different times witch doctors, religious leaders, medical doctors, psychiatrists, psychologists, and social workers have struggled for all or part of the action. We have had a number of caste and class struggles; medical versus nonmedical, professional versus nonprofessional, clinical versus nonclinical staff.

Regardless of the infighting, there has been a fundamental *assumption*, probably pretty much from the beginning, that caregivers have to be highly educated and well-trained experts. Around this central *assumption*, there are a number of *subassumptions*.

1. Universities are the appropriate education facility to train caregivers.
2. Certain educational formats better prepare students to serve emotionally disturbed patients; therefore some professions are better able to serve mental patients.
3. Education and training are the most important factors in producing suitable caregivers.
4. The educational system will produce enough caregivers to serve the potential consumer groups.
5. All treatment should be done by the highly educated professionals.

It should be pointed out that none of these *assumptions* has been supported. Many service organizations would argue that university training is incongruent with the services that we provide our clients. We think that most university departments that are educating professional-service employees show a considerable lag behind service organizations in their concepts of service required.

At our agency many of us have begun to feel that persons educated in the universities are recruited into models of service that make them incompatible with our approach. Persons trained in specialized university departments arrive at our institutions prepared only to function within particular boundaries: talk to the patient, diagnose the patient, plan for the future with the patient, etc. We want staff members who will involve themselves in the patient's total milieu: clothing, eating, cleaning, as well as psychotherapy and diagnosis.

We have evolved toward a position in which we *assume* that the personal equation factor is more important than education. That is, the caregiver's size, personality style, temperament, general intelligence, and other personal characteristics are the prime factors in the emergence of an effective caregiver. This is not to deny the relevance of education to the appropriate person.

Our position has led to the establishment of a career series in which we have moved persons through our system on the basis of personal competence. This, of course, does not prevent persons from moving up in the system through education. A sizable portion of our staff consists of persons with four years of college who have received all their service training at our agency. Those who would say that professionals can deliver services which nonprofessionals cannot must in some way substantiate their position. If we are to support twelve to fifteen years of training, it would seem necessary to substantiate such an expensive, time-consuming enterprise.

## SUMMARY

In summary, there are probably other "great issues," but we feel that in one way or another, we have covered the territory. These are not abstract or isolated issues. How one deploys one's resources is directly related to service goals. The type of service goals, to a great extent, determines the type and quantity of employees and organizational systems. In the long run the consumer suffers as a result of the caregivers' remaining in a rut and refusing to examine their operational systems. In the next chapter, we will begin to examine a new *game plan* with new *assumptions*.

# VI

## The Imprints of History

Through the first five chapters we have been criticizing many of the mainstream patterns in the field of mental health. We are certainly not unique or original in our dissatisfaction with and alienation from most of the current delivery and treatment systems. Glass (1953, 1955), an army psychiatrist, as early as the 1950's reported pioneering mental health service systems that were and still are totally or partially in conflict with mainstream theories and concepts.

Glass had a task different from that of most psychiatrists. He had to treat soldiers who had developed emotional problems in combat and return them to battle. In this task he found the traditional civilian treatment game plan ineffective. Under these circumstances he could have continued to spin his wheels as state hospital administrators did for years or problem-solve a new model. Glass chose the second alternative. He recommended that treatment be performed as close to the battlefield or combat group as possible. He believed that if you removed the soldier to a distant hospital, you minimized his probability of returning. This same principle was not introduced into our agency until 1968 when we entered into a catchment, or geographically oriented, program.

Glass believed treatment should combine "simplicity of procedure with brevity of time." It was vital to his model not to recruit the soldier into a complicated mental health career. He wanted the soldier to see this as a "first aid" experience and not as a lengthy exploration into his past life. Too often civilian patients detour from their mainstream life patterns—work, family, and friends—into a lengthy complicated relationship with a therapist. Therapy should not be an alternative to the patient's social network.

As we were writing this section on Glass's combat approach we remembered an anecdote that he related in a lecture about a year ago. The anecdote is not totally on target but sufficiently close that it is worth relating. We should also point out that we will partially fill in gaps since parts of the anecdote are somewhat vague a year later. It is a story of a young soldier who has just received some bad news. As we remember the story, there was a "Dear John" letter from his girl friend and some other bad news regarding his parents. He felt a little down and developed a headache. He decided that he would go to the dispensary to get some aspirins. When he arrived there a young man on duty asked him about his problems. In the course of the conversation he revealed his several misfortunes and his headache. The young dispensary worker suggested that he see one of the mental health workers (we do not remember what type of professional saw him). As it turned out, he ended up on the mental health "assembly line" which resulted in his being given a social history survey, taking psychological tests, and having a psychiatric evaluation. Toward the end of the day Dr. Glass ran into this young man sitting dejectedly on a bench and asked him why he was dejected. The young soldier related the sequence of events, including the fact that a psychiatric report was being sent to his commanding officer. Dr. Glass asked him what he had learned from this experience. He replied, "To buy my own aspirins." For those who need a happy ending we should report that Dr. Glass saved the day. We can only say that it is a typical story of our mental health times.

As part of maintaining a brief, simple, practical model, Glass felt that it was better to reduce awareness (repression over insight—covering rather than uncovering). He wanted to focus on the here and now problems rather than to trace the soldier's anxieties into the distant past. This latter process is more complicated, endures longer, and is more likely to recruit the soldier into a patient career.

Glass also felt that "success in therapy is largely determined by the degree with which the psychiatrist identifies with the need of the combat group, as opposed to participation with the desires of the individual." This is a particularly interesting principle. It would seem that Glass was aware that the needs of the individual might be at odds with the needs of his combat group and that if he went in that direction, i.e., supported the soldier's needs, it would increase divisiveness and place the soldier in an untenable position vis-à-vis his combat group. It is the same problem that occurs in families when a therapist identifies with the needs of a child rather than with the needs of the family. There seems to be no point in supporting the revolt of a child who is without money or without power. Rather, we have to negotiate a viable relationship with the power people until the child has the resources to accept responsibility for himself.

Certainly one might disagree with Glass's assumptions or axioms. The Armed Forces situation is unique in that one is helping a person reintegrate so that he may return to combat with the subsequent potential death risk. However, from our point of view the crucial variable was Glass's ability to tear loose from existing nonapplicable assumptions and substitute new strategies and tactics that were syntonic with his goals. Glass identified his goals and arrived at solutions that were effective for his purpose. This is an expression of our concept, "treatment through institutional change." We think this is the core of mental health services.

Our game plan, or approach, is certainly not unique or original. Hansell (1967, 1968), Mowrer (1962, 1966a), Caplan (1964), Szasz (1961, 1971), as well as Glass, are only a few examples of original thinkers who have influenced us. These are men who have basically gone counter to the mainstream patterns in the field of mental health. This should in no way imply that these men are necessarily congruent with each other. In this chapter and those which follow we are going to attempt to bring together facets of the developing counter-forces evolving in the field of mental health.


## Brief Historical View

We would like to begin this section with a quotation from an earlier paper by Fisher (1965b): "Psychoanalysis, with its techniques of change, has a recent origin. It is not yet one hundred years old. Compared to the traditional techniques of sociopolitical change which has moved man from despotism to democracy, from slavery to capitalism and from magical religious thinking to modern day Monotheism, it is a 'neonate.' These older systems of social organization played an important role when man was struggling with basic problems of existence: slavery, starvation, uncontrollable rage, patricide and incest. It is unlikely that such problems would have produced psychoanalytical solutions, i.e., turning to insight, understanding and acceptance. When man faces death or the unknown he more likely turns to answers in areas such as magic and religion.

"Psychoanalysis, as a tool of social change, only began as a method to struggle with problems of freedom and satisfaction when the difficulties of dependence, sexual conflicts, and autonomy turned men inward to solve their problems. This became an advanced procedure apparently available to the high resource persons in the society."

It is worth noting that not only is psychoanalysis of recent origin, but the concept, in any form, of mental illness as a disease which needs treatment is at most two hundred years old. We started with the quotation by Fisher to make the point that long before we entered into the mental health business, society had the task of dealing with human problems, maladaptations, and behavioral deviance. Without perspective, we tend to correlate and equate behavioral deviance with mental illness and *assume* that these issues and problems fall only into the province of the caregivers. It will help us to understand that the caregiving professions, state hospitals, clinics, and private therapists represent only one game plan for coping with those problems which we traditionally designate as mental illness.

Prior to the mental health game plan, behavioral deviance was at different times seen to be the "turf" of witch doctors, priests, police forces, the family barbers, and/or God. It is probably not too cynical a remark to state that we would have a difficult time determining which group has been most effective in providing services for the mental health consumer.

As an aside, we would like to make the point that we would not recommend destroying current mental health systems. Some mental health professionals after reading our papers or listening to our lectures assume that we favor eliminating psychologists, social workers, and psychiatrists. This in no way represents our position. It is the narrow view posed by professional mental health workers that we are challenging. In this book we are attempting to widen the perspective by increasing the number of options and game plans available for the consumer. Human problems have to be seen in the context of multiple social systems and not simply as a disease process.

The narrow view of caregivers can be seen in their attitudes about changing human behavior as part of the treatment process. Caregivers or therapists have defined as one of their main tasks the problem of symptom elimination, altering personality, changing values, and/or making behavior "normal." In defining this task for themselves they have tended to characterize this problem as unique to their profession and possible only through their specific technology. In addition, Reik (1946), Reich (1933), Stekel (1950), *et al.*, have tended to attribute a mystical and romantic aura to this change process which has resulted in an enormous mythology about changing human behavior. In actuality, there are numerous professions and individuals who share the task of influencing and altering human systems. Certainly every family unit in raising its children has a considerable preoccupation with molding them. We delight in raising the question with psychologists and psychiatrists as to who knows more about changing behavior—parents or college graduates? It is a question guaranteed to evoke jargon, defensiveness, and circumstantiality. If the professionals consider the possibility that parents may know more, we enjoy asking, How much college credit will you grant for being a parent? The response of the academic people will include terms such as concept formation, theory, true understanding, and ability to generalize. This implies that the parent may change behavior, but he does not really understand what he is doing.

The institution of the family is not the only societal unit involved in changing and molding behavior. Most societies have had educators who have had a mandate to help prepare children to become responsible adults. Perhaps more than any other group they have been obsessed with measuring change in their pupils to substantiate the effectiveness of their educational systems. We are, in effect, making the point that most societies have typically had many different kinds of molders of behavior. In addition to mental health workers we have had families, educators, corrections workers, religious leaders, public relations workers, advertising firms, political leaders, propagandists, employers, employees, etc. The fact is that mental health workers are one of the last professional groups to emerge with this assignment.

To further our perspective, we would like to present several separate quotations from a historical work by Russell (1960). "Social cohesion, during the six and a half centuries from Alexander to Constantine, was secured, not by philosophy and not by ancient loyalties, but by force, first that of armies and then that of civil administration." "Christianity popularized an important opinion, already implicit in the teachings of the stoics, but foreign to the general spirit of antiquity—I mean the opinion that a man's duty to God is more imperative than his duty to the state." "What had happened in the great age of Greece happened again in the Renaissance in Italy: traditional moral restraints disappeared, because they were seen to be associated with superstition; the liberation from fetters made individuals energetic and creative, producing a rare fluorescence of genius; but the anarchy and treachery which inevitably resulted from the decay of morals made Italians collectively impotent, and they fell, like the Greeks, under the domination of nations less civilized than themselves but not so destitute of social cohesion."

We have presented these quotations because we think that the implication of the content approaches the heart of our orientation, or game plan. For example, in the third quotation Russell states that "traditional moral restraints disappeared." He is apparently referring to a reduction in personal and social inhibitions during the Renaissance relating to shifts or alterations in the various social systems. It is, of course, not a new or original observation that the Renaissance was a period of reduced inhibitions as compared to the Dark Ages, or medieval period. We are suggesting that these three quotations from different historical periods refer to changes in morals, the nature of controls, and the individual's relation to the state and God and are reflections of the imprints that different societies had on the members of their communities. Below we are presenting several examples of how different societal attitudes might leave varying imprints on individuals resulting in differing adaptations.

EXAMPLE I

A society which regulates by force probably produces behavior different from that of a society which encourages and educates toward self-control. We see this very much in the concept of "law and order." There are those who would respond to student protests with larger and more active police departments. In contrast there are those who suggest that we attempt to understand the needs which create student protests and consider amending the social system. It is *assumed* that appropriate "establishment" reactions will result in reasonable responses by student groups (self-control).

EXAMPLE II

In state hospitals, where a major task is socializing the patients, there is a continuous struggle between the role of security police (external control) and providing experience opportunities that allow patients to develop their own control. Earlier in the book we discussed the Legislative Visitation Committee that came to investigate our agency. The members of the committee were concerned, distressed, and angry that several of our hospital wards did not meet their expectations for cleanliness and neatness. The Legislative Visitation Committee's attitude brought a major issue into focus.

The ward caregivers who were working with highly regressed patients had been struggling with the problem of how to get these patients to assume responsibility for basic patterns of their lives: clothing themselves, using the bathroom rather than the floor, and maintaining general cleanliness. The staff felt that if patients are treated like helpless incompetents and everything is done for them, it is doubtful that they will ever accept responsibility for their most basic needs. The caregivers were caught in the struggle between meeting what they saw as patient needs and maintaining a public relations posture (which means the staff takes over all the responsibility so that the wards meet the expectancies of outside visitors).

Patients placed in a state hospital society that functions on the security and cleanliness model (law and order) are essentially placed in a vacuum. These patients are not provided with experiences by which people grow. The residents of state institutions are deprived of human experiences such as trust, love, danger, education, pleasure. If it is true that we learn to cope with danger and moral problems through experience, then institutionalized persons will never learn proper adaptations. Placing a person in a sterile society (a vacuum) prevents growth. The institution becomes a warehouse.

We do not want to play historian, nor do we want to bore the reader with a great deal of historical fact, but we do feel that the historical analogue if pursued a little further will aid us in understanding our core concept of "treatment through institutional change." We would like to examine the Renaissance schematically, but we want to identify some characteristics of the period, and consider the experiencing of these characteristics for the persons living in the society.

In general the Renaissance (the "rebirth") is considered the beginning of the modern era. The mental outlook was quite different from that of the medieval period: the church had a diminishing authority, and science an increasing authority. The culture moved from a clerical to a lay orientation. States (nationalism) increasingly replaced the church as the government authority that controlled culture. Feudalism began to recede as the primary economic system (the beginning of the end of serfdom) and to be replaced by capitalism.

Emancipation from the authority of the church led to the growth of individualism, even to the point of anarchy. Discipline—intellectual, moral, and political—was associated in the minds of the men of the Renaissance with the Middle Ages. The moral and political anarchy of fifteenth-century Italy was appalling and gave rise to the doctrines of Machiavelli. This pattern of emancipation, search for freedom, and attack on dogma also set the stage for antiauthoritarian attitudes, agnosticism, and the search for truth through science rather than through religion. Rationality superseded faith, and the pursuit of knowledge became more important than the Word of God.

At the same time, the freedom from mental shackles led to displays of genius in art and literature. These patterns, characteristics of the Renaissance, led to philosophies that were individualistic and subjective. This subjective imprint can be seen in the work of Descartes, Locke, Berkeley, Kant, *et al.*

It is also interesting to speculate whether some of the behavior features that we associate with mental illness, such as withdrawal, creation of private worlds, sensory experiences without stimuli, do not have their genesis in this subjective and antiauthoritarian era.

Why the brief history lesson? We are attempting to increase the reader's sensitivity to the potential impact of a society's institutions, ideologies, and philosophies on the individual. In essence we are saying that the characteristics—traits, values, interests, deviancy, inhibitory systems—of a person born in the midst of the Renaissance are going to be very different from those of someone born in the Middle Ages (probably an era that could be described as the reciprocal of the Renaissance). It is not unfair to say that the characteristic pattern of a historical period is the prime determiner in shaping the man in terms of his positive adaptive patterns as well as of his negative nonadaptive systems. We are attempting to consider the kind of experiences in a historical period that are important in the development of the persons in that society.

To pursue this premise we will look briefly at Machiavelli, a man who was a product of the Renaissance. Machiavelli (1469–1527) was a Florentine, born to a family of average circumstances. Except for a minor post in the Florentine government which he held from 1498 to 1512, he was without work most of his life. His occupational problems began with the restoration of the Medici in 1512. He had always opposed them, so that when they were restored, he was arrested, but acquitted, and allowed to live in retirement in the country near Florence. He became an author for want of another occupation. The impact of his times on him can be seen in his major works *The Prince* and *Discourses*. We will examine his ideologies and philosophies briefly. In *The Prince,* he is concerned with discovering from history and from contemporary events how principalities are won, how they are held, and how they are lost. This concern was part of the spirit of the times. Most rulers were not legitimate and probably gained power in the same corrupt fashion by which Hitler succeeded. Machiavelli was intrigued by the means by which rulers such as Cesare Borgia pursued their ambitions. Machiavelli, who was intimately acquainted with the villainies of Borgia, sums it up: "Reviewing thus all the actions of the duke [Cesare], I find nothing to blame; on the contrary, I feel bound, as I have done, to hold him as an example to be imitated by all who by fortune and with the aims of others have risen to power."

We will present below a number of the attitudes, beliefs, and values of Machiavelli.

1. He had great admiration for skill and actions that lead to fame.
2. He would not expect such a work to be undertaken from unselfish motives, but from love of power and still more of fame.
3. Power is for those who have the skill to seize it in a free competition.
4. The best constitution is one that apportions legal rights among princes, nobles, and people in proportion to their real power.
5. In a chapter that is entitled "In What Way Princes Must Keep Faith," he, in effect, suggests they should keep faith when it pays to do so, but not otherwise. A prince must on occasion be faithless.
6. "If the end is held good, we must choose means adequate to its achievement."

Machiavelli's philosophy and political ideologies are clearly a reflection of his time. The fact is that he approximates the role of a reporter who is accurately detailing the spirit of the Renaissance. It is clear from his theories that he values individual skill, respects power, and makes assumptions that are subjective in nature; e.g., power belongs to the person who earns it —there are no true external criteria for determining who should hold power.

Machiavelli could not have been produced in the Middle Ages, although the seeds of the Renaissance were generated by the maladaptation ideologies and institutions of the medieval era: rigid dogmas, corruption in the church, and the exploitation of the people. He clearly was produced by the dynamics of the Renaissance. Erikson (1958) in his biography of Luther portrays in detail the dynamics of an era on a man. Erikson mediates the impact of the historical times through the institution of Luther's family, particularly his father.

Perhaps, with the Machiavellian historical analogue in mind, it might be useful to consider the role of the superintendent in a state mental hospital and the impact of the superintendent on his agency. An examination of the forces, vectors, and influences relating to this caregiver will aid us in understanding the system. In most state systems the superintendents of state hospitals are medical doctors. This is true although their work responsibilities are totally administrative. In fact, we cannot think of one single advantage in having a medical superintendent. As most readers know, general hospitals typically do not have physicians as directors. This is not to deny that some physicians are excellent administrators, but this is probably a personal equation factor totally unrelated to their education. To the credit of the Department of Mental Health in Illinois it employs superintendents from different professions, and we would say that rankings in regard to competence would have nothing to do with profession.

We have had an interesting regression recently in regard to

type of profession and superintendent's position, in that the salaries of medical superintendents were increased over those of nonmedical superintendents. Both kinds of men perform the same duties, duties that have nothing to do with medicine, and yet one group receives a higher salary. The pressure to maintain medical control over human problems is unrelenting.

Superintendents, regardless of profession, have no security. They are appointed by the director of the Department of Mental Health without contract, tenure, or civil service status. They can be fired on the spot without cause by the director. Their only security can come from political friends or from developing a loyal constituency among their employees which would be willing to stand by them, and if necessary, walk out to support them. These protective systems will make the director think before he stirs up a potential hornet's nest. We should point out that superintendents typically do not develop these protective screens and yet most do not get fired. A superintendent soon learns the survival game plan, i.e., a person in this role is typically conservative, careful, and resistive to change. A surviving superintendent must develop a sensitivity to danger. He will have a true "third ear" that supersedes anything Reik has described. His "third ear" is being constantly tested and evaluated. If Reik is wrong, no one ever knows, but if the superintendent's "third ear" is off, he will soon be looking for a new job.

The man chosen to lead the hospital is forced to serve his director rather than the consumers or his employees. The director of the Department of Mental Health is in the cabinet of the governor and is subject to all the political pressures to which any cabinet member is subject. The director's job is obviously dependent upon the good will of the governor. If the governor decides that a department must reduce expenditures, it becomes the task of the director to justify the governor's need or resign. If he chooses to support the governor, the superintendent must justify the reductions or resign. If during this time a superintendent for good reasons developed a program to rejuvenate the hospital that would increase the budget, he could be fired or simply ridiculed. Financial expenditures are political, not an expression of a system need.

The superintendent is a key person in the system of a hospital. As the system exists, if he is to survive, he must, like Machiavelli, be a reflection of his time. It becomes an important therapeutic question whether he should function more in the clinical context or in the political context. If we choose the former, we have to decrease his vulnerability. If we support the political framework, we leave the system as it is. The major point being made is that these questions reflect more vital issues than the struggles over treatment techniques.

When we begin to consider the impact of overall system dynamics on the role of the individual—e.g., the hospital superintendent and the philosophies of Machiavelli—the comparative influence of mental health therapies is much like a pimple on an elephant. Each historical period through its social systems and institutions sets the structure for the development of the individual and the delineation of his characteristics. In earlier sections of the book we have attempted to describe the impact of one institution, the state hospital, on its residents. Our main focus in serving the residents was to alter the institution ("treatment through institutional change"): changing staff attitudes, redefining roles, upgrading the physical environment, altering organization, etc.

At the core of the theme "treatment through institutional change" is the belief that societal systems are organized around elaborate reward and punishment systems. The society is organized around the administration of these values. If your society focuses on law and order themes, you are much more likely to have one man at the top making all the decisions (authoritarian model). In the custodial state hospital the superintendent is a one-man operation—he might have a conservative business manager as his only confidant. As the hospital becomes more treatment-oriented, there is the development of a much broader base of power with great increases in delegation of authority, power, and responsibility.

The built-in values of the society mold our behavior and leave the various imprints of its institutions on each citizen. Behavior that is valued is rewarded and increases esteem (feelings of well-being). Behavior that is contrary to the values of a society is punished and leads to loss of esteem. Out of this orientation, one of the major service techniques has emerged for clinical services. For example, at our agency we have become sensitized to the built-in rewards and punishments extant in our systems. The analysis of our value systems led to organizational changes that resulted in growth experiences for our residents. It would seem clear in retrospect that the values of the hospital in the '50s supported regression and prolonged institutionalization.

In the 1950's staff often referred to patients they liked as "good patients." These were the patients who were quiet, did everything they were asked, showed deference to ward staff, and always knew their place. These residents received all the goodies that were available: grounds passes, coffee and cigarettes, home visits, private rooms, etc. In effect, these patients were rewarded for identifying with their keepers and the institution. It was an implicit system for recruiting reasonably inadequate persons into an institutional way of life. For years, it was these "good patients" who provided many of the hospital's necessary lower echelon services. We assume that all societies mold behavior in this fashion.

We will complete this section with one final historical analogue. This analogue might help the reader to understand further the reward and punishment model and its relationship to "treatment through institutional change." It would seem clear that very different reward and punishment systems existed in the Renaissance than in the Middle Ages. In the latter period, the church had primary control of available tokens (reward and punishment). Earthly rewards were deferred for good post-death placement. We literally had a prescribed step system for entry into heaven with earthly witnesses to point the way. In the Renaissance, the state held the tokens and passed them out for earthly accomplishments. A man's ability to create, win and seize power, and wage war became highly valued and was greatly rewarded. We assume, with considerable historical justification, that the different models of reward and punishment produced different characteristics in the citizens of the Middle Ages than in those of the Renaissance.

## RECAPITULATION AND IMPLICATIONS
### OF HISTORICAL PERSPECTIVE

This would be a good place to restate our objection to the medical model. People come to mental health caregivers with almost an infinite variety of problems: no money, no friends, no place to live, no one likes them, they have headaches, they have nowhere else to go, they have ulcers, etc. To force all such persons into one assembly line is a crime of major proportions. To assume that so many different problems have only one solution system is an insult to the intelligence of all caregivers. The Medical-Freudian solution has forced everyone who needs human service help to act sick, give up their sense of responsibility, and to stop determining their own destiny.

In this chapter we have been attempting to make the point that human beings require a variety of experiences for growth. These experiences vary with historical periods, age, sex, geographical location, needs, etc. In line with this broad perspective it seems incredibly simple to conclude that human beings can only overcome maladaptations within the context of the disease model in the hands of a physician. In context with these remarks it was interesting to hear Dr. Jerome Jaffe, the President's Director for Drug Abuse, quoted on a recent news broadcast to the effect that religion has helped more addicts than methadone. Dr. Jaffe has long been an advocate of methadone as a treatment technique for heroin addicts.

In the spirit of the medical-hospital orientation, there has been an insistence that physicians administer programs relating to those behavioral problems which are characterized as mental illness. In most residential mental health facilities physicians have control over patients' expenditure of funds, the issuing of privileges to patients, determining whether a patient should be restrained, or any number of human service activities that are not medical problems. We are suggesting that there may on occasion be medical factors in these decisions, but this is rare or the exception to the rule. We are not by any stretch of the imagination implying that for certain human growth experiences a physician may not be useful. We are stating that for different persons different experiences and a variety of human beings are necessary to growth—the "turf" does not belong to any one group.

In most states there is a constant power struggle between medical societies and other professions in regard to responsibility for the mentally ill. The State of Illinois began relenting on this medical orientation in 1963 with great benefit to the hospital patient. This has been an important factor in the improvement of the Department of Mental Health in the 1960's.

A system should reflect the needs of the consumers and not the power needs of the employees. Recognition of and response to the needs of the consumer is at the heart of the service approach. If a person arrives at our door in need of "first aid" counseling, marital counseling, and financial help, we should respond to these needs. It is not necessary to explore his blood chemistry, his urine, and the condition of his lungs.

The medical model molds sickness and it rewards those behavioral patterns which reflect sickness. If you are sick, you can be excused from responsibility with dignity. But it is not a problem-solving system; instead, it forces the therapist to be the "poor" patient's problem solver. We have to ask if this constitutes the appropriate environment for those persons who have trouble coping with their surroundings.

## DEVELOPING NEW OPTIONS

The basic task in the mental health field is to design game plans or service models that will meet the needs of those persons in the community who have developed maladaptive solutions to their needs. In order to develop new options, there are certain issues that will have to be identified. We will list these below and in the final two chapters discuss them in detail along with developing options for service.

### Identification of Needs

We feel that at the heart of all human service programs there must be an understanding of the basic human needs. We will suggest several models for consideration.

### Identification of Target Population

We have to widen our concept of the type of problems that need service from caregivers. It is unrealistic to think that the only true patients are the ones who have traditionally sought psychoanalysis.

### Analysis of the Society

It is important to understand our various systems (family, educational, and social) and study the impact of these systems on the individual. At this point in history we are in no position to modify our systems in order to aid the individual with his problems, even if we had the power, because we do not know what experiences are necessary for the growth of the individual.

### Develop New Community Caregiver Role

Just as the role of the caregiver has been radically altered in the hospital, so it has to be changed in the community. Caregivers have to develop a more extensive generalist role vis-à-vis the consumer.

### CASE PRESENTATION

We would like to end this chapter with a brief case description.

### Background Material

A forty-one-year-old white, middle-class woman with three children (her husband earns about $20,000 a year) reports that approximately five years ago she became "mentally ill." Her primary symptom is loss of feelings: "I cannot even tell when I have to go to the bathroom. I don't know how I feel anymore. I have no sexual feelings." The overall behavioral configuration appears to be that of a deeply depressed person: four suicide attempts, loss of appetite, constipation, retardation in speech and movement, general loss of motivation. During the last five years she has spent the majority of her time in residential facilities.

The client feels that her "illness" began when she was thirty years old with a gradually increasing depression which overwhelmed her and resulted in her finally being hospitalized at the age of thirty-six. During the period from thirty to thirty-six her husband went into business for himself, and he was rarely around the house. They also had their third child during this time—definitely an unwanted child. The theme of these five years is the absence of the husband, increasing responsibilities, and mounting depression. The first hospitalization was precipitated by a suicide attempt.

## *"Treatment" Background*

From ages thirty-six to forty-one (the period of an identifiable "illness"), she was a resident in one of the better-known treatment facilities in the Midwest. She had innumerable electric shock treaments, antidepressant drugs, psychoanalysis, the entire repertoire of therapies used in servicing the depressed patient, yet at this point in her life she is in a state hospital, has been abandoned by her family, and has given up hope for the future.

## *Interview and General Thoughts*

The thumbnail sketch presented above emerged from the interview. The client feels that everyone has been fair to her and that caregivers have done everything humanly possible. Perhaps some paraphrased dialogue will give the reader insight into her life-style.

CLIENT: The situation is hopeless. They have done everything and none of my feelings have come back.

INTERVIEWER: What have they done?

CLIENT: They gave me shock treatment, experimental drugs, psychotherapy—just everything. Nothing helped and nothing will ever help.

INTERVIEWER (*almost challenging*): Are you saying that if someone dedicated themselves to bringing your feelings back, it would do no good?

CLIENT: It is useless; they have tried everything.

INTERVIEWER: It seems to me they have hardly tried anything. When you think of all the ways people manage depression in their personal lives, your therapists have hardly tried anything.

CLIENT: I don't understand what you mean.

INTERVIEWER: Well, everyone has some depression and each person utilizes different experiences to overcome these feelings. There are people who eat their way out of depression;

others seek solutions in wine, and still others turn to sex.
Have you tried to work out a personal solution?
CLIENT: No, they have tried everything.

We have found this case interesting because it demonstrates
the limitation of thinking when one stays with one model.
There was no question in our minds that if it were possible to
open the entire repertoire of human experiences to this client,
she would find it impossible to remain depressed. There are
many everyday vital life forces with which we can service our
clients if we escape the limitations of our own theories and
models. It is these everyday vital experiences that allow most
of us to overcome the immobilizing inner anxieties and depres-
sions. The broad historical excursion in this chapter is an attempt to widen the perspective of the reader.

# VII

## Modules of Experience: To Grow or Not to Grow

We would like to begin with a quotation from Chapter I of this book. The quotation is in reference to the psychoanalytical client. "The clients who do have a good prognosis have very specific qualities. They must be sufficiently tied into the cash economy that they can afford a significant cash outlay—a minimum of two thousand dollars per year. This usually indicates well-developed occupational skills, a 'successful' marriage, and/or wealthy relatives. The therapy model demands an articulate person who is able to mature through this kind of experience. A typical client is middle class, verbal, most likely a female, above average in intelligence, and diagnosed neurotic."

We have recalled the above quotation to suggest that the psychoanalytical game plan possibly provides certain persons with experiential opportunities which allow them to grow, to become increasingly effective and adaptive in their surroundings. That is, it is possible that the experiences and technology which are part of psychoanalysis (insight, transference, free association, interpretation, and probes into the unconscious) initiate processes between two persons that allow either one, therapist or client, or both to become more adaptive and effective in living in their milieu.

We would like to sensitize our readers to the concept that

every society provides or makes available to people "modules of experience" which have potential maturational force for its citizens. This is clearer in regard to the opportunities we attempt to make available to children. The classic example of this concept is the "school elevator." A child enters the school system usually at five years of age, and depending upon his motivation and skills, can utilize this "module of experience" as a developmental option to emerge at a higher socioeconomic level.

It is important to remember that not all "modules of experience" represent growth opportunities for all members of the society. We know that schools are utilized much more effectively by white middle-class children than by black lower-class children. In fact, schools probably play a major role in manufacturing and maintaining the *status quo* of the society. For example, we have the situation that if a person goes through an exclusive private school system and graduates from Harvard, he is considered to have the credentials for a "high station" in life. Yet he probably cannot pursue this educational pattern unless he has considerable funds and certain early-developed attitudes.

In most cultures, the primary "modules of experience" reflect the mainstream pattern of the society. The American society has provided multiple chances for growth, but these opportunities are primarily accessible to persons who have those resources which link them into the mainstream. We have not traditionally provided options for minorities, for lower socioeconomic groups, for persons who are variously handicapped, for women, for retarded persons, for eccentrics, etc. It is from these persecuted, scapegoated, and alienated people that we have filled our public-aid rolls, prisons, mental hospitals, addiction agencies, and alcoholic programs. Most agencies who serve these individuals have maximized security models and minimized developmental services. These relationships with service agencies have been dehumanizing, further alienating, and destructive to the human spirit.

To understand the concept of "modules of experience" more clearly, it might be useful to scrutinize briefly the American culture as we did the Renaissance in the last chapter. We are not attempting to identify abnormalities in the culture or to point out what is wrong; rather, we want to report on what we see. In effect, we want to understand the "modules of experience" that this society makes available to its citizens.

## AMERICAN PATTERNS: "MODULES OF EXPERIENCE"

We do know that most of the early inhabitants of the United States were white Anglo-Saxon Protestants (WASPs) who brought their values, ideologies, and beliefs with them: Protestant ethics, Renaissance spirit, and secular authority. At the time people began to leave Europe, they were highly influenced by the rising tide of the Reformation and the Renaissance. The Western world was challenging existing rules, laws, dogmas, and beliefs. In fact, the theories of anarchy emerge from this era. During the next four centuries we have the development of laissez-faire economics, egalitarianism, science, the French philosophies, the Encyclopedists, the era of revolutions, the theory of evolution, mass education, Marxian communism, Freudian theories, and the industrial revolution.

These forces and the American western frontier came together as "modules of experience" to create an American character. The American character is expressed in a series of myths, fantasies, beliefs, and values. Any person living in the United States can become anything he desires (the Horatio Alger myth). Whatever a man earns through his own efforts, he should be allowed to retain. We have implicitly accepted the survival of the fittest philosophy. We have tended to admire successful persons even when they are literally bandits—the James brothers. The successful exploiters of the nineteenth century—Rockefeller, Vanderbilt, Carnegie, etc.—have become legends. Ayn Rand in her two novels *The Fountainhead* and *Atlas Shrugged* is extremely effective in detailing the thinking and values of this era.

Certainly through most of the nineteenth century and a good deal of the twentieth century, we have believed in a nonplanning society in which the natural competitive patterns would create a style of life desired by its citizens. Success in this culture supposedly reflected individual competence, and failure in the society meant incompetence and some basic weakness in the individual's makeup. It became important to present a good front because this, in effect, was your "report card." The need to achieve success would become sufficiently intense that any means (shades of Machiavelli) were acceptable. To characterize this society briefly, we will utilize the following one-liners.

1. Materialistic rather than spiritual
2. Competitive rather than cooperative
3. A nonplanning society
4. Inconsistent and capable of being viewed as hypocritical
5. Very goal-oriented
6. Pragmatic and practical
7. Almost anything is ethical in regard to selling products
8. External appearances are important
9. May the best man win
10. Action-oriented, with some tendency to avoid deep thinking
11. Anxiety-ridden, with great need for tranquilizers (alcohol, aspirins, narcotics, Thorazine, etc.)

It might be noted that some of the characteristics are inconsistent with one another. It is this exact type of inconsistency that is part of the American pattern. It is a society that can be idealistic and at the same time "super" practical. This culture has been remarkably good to the "winners," but there has been a tendency to ignore and alienate the "losers." For the most part, "losers" have been extruded into community "snake pits," the ghettos.

There have been moderating influences in regard to the pure early American philosophy that we have been examining. Barry Goldwater was probably the last Presidential candidate to support a position congruent with the above philosophy. He and the author Ayn Rand, who are both proponents of this position, appear to have trouble dealing with "losers" in the society. When we attempt to cope with the issues and problems of the alienated and the handicapped, we may be forced to reconsider basic societal institutions and systems.

In order to clarify this situation, we can begin by examining those individuals designated as the "plus" persons, or "winners," in our culture. These are the bright, competitive individuals who have everything going for them: mainstream family, good resources, proper "up-beat" motivation, excellent physical characteristics, and a likable temperament. An individual such as this grooves into our system and manages to obtain excellent payoffs for all his efforts. The culture is organized to support this person. If things do happen to go wrong for the "plus" person and stresses become unmanageable, the "first aid" or therapeutic intervention techniques are designed so that this type of client can maximize their use.

In contrast, if we examine a societal "minus" person, or a "loser," i.e., an individual from the ghetto, with few resources, lack of mainstream motivation, uneducated, apathetic, unattractive, and moody, we find that the community is organized to punish him. He does poorly in school, and it becomes a nightmare for the unsuccessful student. If he is able to obtain a job, it is typically an uninteresting, poor paying, overly demanding position. When the stresses become overly taxing, he is usually extruded to an institution that is organized around security themes rather than growth forces. Even though the society is not his "cup of tea," he is expected to live within the moral systems, values, and ethics that have been forged to maintain the *status quo*.

Therapists have had the audacity to try to deal with these

"minus" persons by designating them as mentally ill and attempting to "cure" them. This meant that the therapist was attempting to "rip off" the only protection and pleasure the individual had. We approach a forty-year-old man who has no resources, no career, no family, and no education and insist that he stop drinking. We do not provide alternatives other than occasional conversations with a therapist. Given this man's life, perhaps drinking is the best option available. Suppose we altered the options and the alcoholic would have a choice each day: a hundred dollars, a beautiful girl, or a bottle of whiskey. In that event, there might be changes in selection. The "minus" people are frequently in a position where the seeming maladaptation may be the best option or solution. We would think that it might be an interesting experience to see if we could buy away mental illness. That is, offer large appropriate rewards to patients to give up symptoms, change their behavior, or leave the hospital.

## Bringing Together Some Developing Themes

At this point we feel that it is useful to bring several of our themes together. A community molds the behavior of its citizens through its built-in reward and punishment patterns. Each culture differentiates through this process a distribution of citizens, with highly "plus" persons at one end and highly "minus" persons at the other end of the distribution. The potential growth modules in a society are designed to benefit the "plus" individuals and at the same time support the *status quo*. Even the therapy models reflect the needs of the "plus" persons, and generally "minus" people are said to have a poor prognosis for treatment. In our culture, few "minus" persons (we refer to them as the "disadvantaged" or "high-risk" clients) are rescued by traditional mental health systems. In fact, it would seem impossible to rescue the alienated person by therapy models designed for the mainstream citizens.

Generally prisons, state hospitals, and various other "Devil's Island" institutions have been informally designed as the "educational" facilities for "societal losers." Caregivers with carefully prepared blinders, working in these agencies, have ignored the destructive surroundings and minimal options and have attempted to deliver a "medicine" to "cure" them of their "disease." What is this "disease" that physicians have been asked to "cure"? The "minus" persons have not been able to groove into the community's systems, institutions, and values. They have refused to accept their "place" in the community. For this failure, the mainstream of society assaults them as "sick." In turn, the disadvantaged individuals with few available resources respond with their limited weapons (withdrawal, apathy, violence, irrationality, and suicide) which we label as schizophrenia, psychopathy, hebephrenia, etc. Armed with these labels, led by physicians, we have launched an attack: psychosurgery, Metrazol, insulin, and electricity. We are going to "cure" them or exile them for life. They are to be packaged our way or be retained out of sight.

If this behavior is a disease, then flunking French is a disease, divorce is a disease, and being fired from a job is a disease. It is our feeling that this kind of thinking and the current Medical-Freudian technology for overcoming alienation and aiding the disadvantaged to return to the mainstream have not been productive. In fact, as we have indicated, "modules of experience" such as psychoanalysis, public education, and medical treatment (lobotomies, shock therapy, hydrotherapy, etc.) have probably become counterproductive.

Although communities do not organize to produce antimainstream "modules of experience," such events do occasionally erupt. Probably the more open and more permissive societies are more likely to have the latitude and tolerance for meaningful countertrends. The labor movement in the 1930's became such a "module of experience" for many alienated persons. Many workers used the labor movement as a career series that provided them with a reentry link into the mainstream.

In our current affairs, there has probably been no more exciting growth experience than the civil rights movement. History is dotted with such "turn on" events: emergence of great religious leaders, antislavery movements, etc.

Typically, these "experiential modules" have great initial excitement, achieve rapport with a group of alienated persons, then become formalized, lose their excitement, and become another sterile institution. There is no question in our minds that public education and psychoanalysis began an exciting change system only later to become formalized, closed, and, to a great extent, sterile.

We are obviously recommending that caregivers must involve themselves in the task of creating, supporting, and increasing the number of "experience modules" available to their consumers. We feel that this is particularly true in regard to their consumers who are labeled as "high risk," or disadvantaged. In this task we are not comparing caregivers to Gandhi, Martin Luther King, or Jesus Christ, but we feel that within their sphere of influence or within the limitations of their power base, they can bring about changes that will result in "treatment through institutional change." This demands new perspectives, new philosophies, new goals, and new opportunities. To those who feel we have been nihilistic and opposed to the caregiving professions, it should become clear that the enterprises we are suggesting go well beyond anything that caregivers have traditionally considered their territory.

It is not our purpose to substitute new institutions for old institutions. New systems rather quickly become old systems with a subsequent loss of vitality. We are interested in initiating processes that are open, ongoing, and continuously changing. Any good teacher knows that everything he is teaching is incorrect—time will prove that, and in a sense, it is his task to establish a process whereby next year's lectures will have superseded current material. An instructor should be encouraging his students to criticize and tear his concepts apart.

When Freud first introduced psychoanalytical observations regarding incest, infantile sexuality, and man's irrational motivations, these were exciting observations that sparked a meaningful process. However, his followers decided that these were ultimate truths by which we all had to live. It is this attitude that is "killing" psychoanalysis.

Man becomes stupid when he is ruled by his theories, concepts, and "great truths." It has been, and is, the tyranny of obsolete mental health theories that led and leads caregivers down stupid pathways. It is amazing and horrifying to observe theoretical beliefs short-circuiting the brain and common sense.

EXAMPLE I

The first example of stupidity takes place on a state hospital ward. This is considered a progressive ward that is no longer functioning in the medical model. The ward uses the human service approach. The caregivers' basic attitude is that everybody should be treated the same. Therapy, except for chemotherapy, is nonspecific. Everyone is expected to be responsible for cleaning the ward and working in the rehabilitation workshop. On the traditional ward, special treatment plans are developed for each patient. The ward in question, for good reasons, we think, did not follow the prescriptive approach. There were, of course, many patients who objected to this one-model orientation, but they were typically persuaded to function within the system. Generally this nonspecific model works satisfactorily. One day a very determined young man arrived on the ward. In previous pressure situations he had killed his mother and deliberately cut off his arm with a saw. You would think that the staff would consider him a determined individual and take special precautions. In any event, they placed him under the same pressure situation as other patients and he responded in his own special way. He set fire to the ward.

EXAMPLE II

A second example of caregiver stupidity involves an analyst treating a young woman who was a surgeon by profession. She was the daughter of an imposing man, and in the analytical sessions a good deal of the content related to her relationship with her father. In analytic terminology she was confused in regard to identification issues and Oedipal problems. The analyst became caught up in the "lovely" dynamics and even after the patient reported surgically removing one breast, he continued the series of discussions. She, of course, removed the second breast while he continued in his theoretical reveries.

The mental health field has many anecdotes relating to individual caregiver brain lapses and to the stupidity of hospitals and entire departments. We attempted to portray aspects of this stupidity in Chapters II and III in the case history of our agency.

## A DEVELOPMENTAL PERSPECTIVE: NECESSARY "MODULES OF EXPERIENCE"

We are not presenting this material in order to make available a detailed account of developmental theory. The fact is that we are primarily restating developmental themes from Chapter I in terms of a new perspective. For the reader who would like to pursue the themes of this section in detail, we would suggest reading the following authors: Freud (1964), Erikson (1950), Piaget (1932), Klein (1932), Bower (1960), and Fisher (1965a). Our focus in this section is on the "modules of experience" necessary for the organism's growth. That is, we are taking this detour to establish a developmental analogue for the two concepts of "modules of experience" and "treatment through institutional change."

It is assumed by the writers listed above that humans in the process of development, or maturation, pass through a series of stages, or positions. There are differences in opinion in regard to the significance of heredity and environment—some writers focusing on heredity and some emphasizing environment. However, at this juncture this is not a vital issue. In any event, it is believed that at each of these stages there are certain crucial problems which have to be resolved or worked through. There are differences in opinion as to what can be designated as the crucial issues, but they vary around concepts such as trust, autonomy, acceptance of external control, self-control, identification, and separation. It becomes society's task to provide the "modules of experience" that allow the organism to grow and develop the capacity to master the problems of each position. Most theorists, particularly Erikson, assume that each stage has a crisis (peaked anxiety) in which the maturing person has the opportunity to resolve the crisis by stepping back (regression), remaining fixed, or moving ahead to a more advanced stage.

How the individual responds to these various stages is to a great extent determined by the "modules of experience" made available. This varies with countries, cultures, socioeconomic groups, ethnic groups, and racial groups. The differences are related to family composition, the designated responsible institutions, attitudes about child-rearing (breast-feeding, toilet-training, disciplining, degree of permissiveness, etc.), the educational system, religious patterns, attitudes about sex and hostility, interests, values, and intelligence.

It is believed that all adults have their lives colored by certain positions, or stages, which were especially pleasurable or frustrating. For any historical period or any specific culture, certain stages are considered to be more influential in providing them with a special flavor.

We assume that at each position of development, depending upon the nature of the issues and the available experiences for handling the issues, the seeds of various skills, interests, traits, and values are planted. To explain this more fully, we will examine a Freudian assumption. It is part of the Freudian developmental theory that a child during his second year becomes involved with his parents in the issue of toilet-training. Analysts believe that certain patterns relating to decision-making, autonomy, trust, and education are determined by the interaction of the parents and the infant in the toilet-training experience. Certainly these relationships have never been scientifically established; however, as a general concept, it does seem possible, if not probable, that inappropriate early "modules of experience" will interfere with, though not halt, certain traits, skills, values, etc., from emerging later in life. These experiential failures may lay the groundwork for future problems; e.g., there appears to be evidence that the "seeds" for becoming a good student are planted prior to the child's entry in school. In fact, there have been preschool programs introduced for disadvantaged persons based on this assumption. However, we are not sure how, when, and who should plant these "seeds." There are many questions relating to observable abilities, interests, values, and skills and the conditions for their development. What experiences make a person religious? Why does a child at five years of age demonstrate a careerlike interest in music? Why does a child develop an interest in mathematics? There are an endless number of such questions.

Although we have little scientific knowledge in this area, everyone has strong opinions. Every mother rears her child within her own set of prejudices. If the mothers run into difficulty, they go to an "expert" and he provides his prejudices. Recently we have had political figures attacking permissiveness as a child-rearing tactic, and we suppose that Spiro Agnew has as much right to his opinion as Sigmund Freud and Benjamin Spock have for their stances.

The problems become increasingly compounded when an adult seeks help in regard to adjustment difficulties, skill development, lack of education, marital failures, and/or career concerns. We do not know why the issue developed. It is improbable, if not impossible, to identify early deprivation problems that may have caused the current maladjustments. Even if we identified early experiential deprivations that set the stage for the current situation, we cannot be sure that the omitted experience, if made available now, would allow the person to regroup and begin to grow again. Generally, if a person seeks help for a difficulty, caregivers offer psychotherapy as the "wild card" mechanism for all of man's adjustment problems. As we pointed out earlier, this is a very limited approach.

## PRINCIPLES OF "TREATMENT THROUGH INSTITUTIONAL CHANGE"

In Chapter III, we described the efforts of a state hospital to reconstitute itself through the principle of "treatment through institutional change." This means that the institution reorganized, developed new philosophies and ideologies, and altered its environment in an effort to provide its residents with new "modules of experience." These change patterns are presented in Figure 1.

Out of these therapeutic experiences, we developed certain principles that influenced and organized our operation.

1. The great change forces in altering our patients are environmental or sociological.
2. We *assumed* that it was best not to remove the individual from his usual surroundings. Service should be provided as close to home as possible.
3. Residential services should be retained as a last-ditch measure.
4. The services of the state hospital should be delivered in

# THERAPEUTIC REORGANIZATION

Figure 1

| NEEDS | APPROACHES |
| --- | --- |
| Allow patients to participate in the process of improving their living conditions | Introduction of Jones & Cumming & Cumming milieu therapy programs in 1961 |
| Provide greater flexibility, expedite change, and increase innovations | Decentralization of the hospital into Unit System in 1963 |
| Increase patient-staff contacts regarding counseling, problem-solving, and planning | Beginning of the team approach in 1965, with staff being allocated to programs rather than departments |
| Provide wide range of services to maximum number of patients | Development of the generalist philosophy in 1965 and the introduction of the career series—this has only begun to peak in the last year or two |
| Increase accountability for patient service, attempt to give all patients "some of the action" (no decline option), increase DMH service to community | Development of Subzone System in 1968, utilizing catchment-territorial concepts |
| Optimal utilization of personnel, eliminate poor physical plant and equipment, provide increased services to infirmary and geriatric patients, and upgrade and standardize and increase services at admission point | Various reorganizations reflecting a change of the hospital status:<br>1. Closing down of redundant services and discontinuing use of obsolete buildings<br>2. Uniting Geriatrics and Infirmaries<br>3. Establishing a new Central Admission Service<br>4. Construction of new physical plants<br>5. Implementation of increased community services |

terms of the everyday living experiences and not through a separate technology, such as psychotherapy.

5. All patients should get an equal share of the services.
6. Discharge is the goal for all residents.
7. The generalist employee was most valuable in the state hospital.
8. A career ladder available to both patients and staff is valuable in creating meaningful motivation.
9. People should be assessed in terms of competency and personal equation factors rather than past credentials.
10. The concept of extrusion or exiling should be eliminated.
11. The staff should expect patients to function like other citizens.
12. Changing the behavior rather than the inner man should be emphasized.

These twelve principles concretely reflect the concept of "treatment through institutional change" and, we assume, result in new experiences for the residents of a state hospital. In Chapter VI, we described some of Glass's (1955) themes of combat psychiatry which in effect reflect another approach of "treatment through institutional change" and new "modules of experience."

We would like to conclude this chapter with a case history that we feel will help delineate the concepts of "modules of experience" and "treatment through institutional change" through yet another perspective.

CASE PRESENTATION

### Identifying Material

The client is a young, unmarried, white woman. At present she is twenty-five years old. She is a rather bright person (her I.Q. is around 125), but if you knew her only superficially, you would tend to underestimate her intelligence. She is not articulate, blocks easily, and does not have easy access to her inner feelings and thoughts. She graduated from high school and sporadically takes college courses (at this point her college credits would be equivalent to a semester's work). She has generally been employed in semiskilled positions; i.e., she has been trained by the organizations that employed her. For the remainder of the case presentation, we will call her Joan.

### Background Material

Joan was the younger child in a family of two children. Her family was in the lower socioeconomic levels. The mother and the father were rather old when the children were born. In fact, the father, a railroad man, retired soon after Joan's birth. The brother was eight years older than the patient. During the eighteen years that Joan lived in the house, there was a steady deterioration in the family structure.

The father was the dominant member of the household and ruled in an authoritarian manner. After he retired, he became a heavy drinker, if not an alcoholic. He bullied everyone in the house and psychologically destroyed the brother. Joan was his favorite, but he would periodically make sexual advances toward her. However, she was the only one in the family who would stand up to him, and she resisted his advances.

The mother spent most of her formative years in a mental retardation facility. She was certainly not a mentally retarded person. It was more a function of her social circumstances, her psychologically reduced functioning, and her external appearance that led to her long institutionalization. There is no question that the long institutionalization left its mark on her personality. Most of the time she was passive, but periodically she became impulsive and raging and would accuse Joan of involving herself sexually with the father. After the father's retirement, the mother joined him in his alcoholic career, leaving the household and the children to their own devices.

The brother, Joe, was very bright, but by all accounts he

was extremely disturbed. There were times when he dressed like a woman, and at other times he made sexual advances toward Joan. His role toward his sister varied from the sexual advances, which she resisted, to acting like a bullying father, which she rejected.

Rather early in her development, she was thrust into the role of trying to hold things together. She would clean the house, cook the meals, and gather up her drunken mother and father at the bar and bring them home. As she relates the story, it is difficult to imagine why she did not disintegrate. Most "modules of experience" that are available to and considered necessary for children in their process of development appeared to be absent. Expressions of love were perverted or unavailable. Discipline and structure in any consistent fashion were absent. There were no obvious figures with whom she could identify. The house they lived in disintegrated along with the family, so that even the physical environment was intolerable. Despite these horrendous surroundings, she did complete school, did not take on those patterns of behavior considered psychotic, and when she reached the age of eighteen, had the sense to leave home and seek her fortune.

## The Treatment Era

She moved about one hundred miles from her home. In terms of her parents' lack of mobility, this was as good as a thousand miles. This decision, which was the first of several steps in totally separating herself from the family, is an excellent example of "treatment through institutional change." No one advised her to do this, but it led to a final separation from a malignant family situation (the break from a major community institution).

In this attempt to build a new life, she obtained a civil service position that had considerable security. She was able to live on the grounds of her place of employment and receive board for a small amount of money. If she spent her salary impulsively, she did not have to worry about her basic existence. This was a fortunate arrangement for a young girl who was totally without external resources, and who needed some opportunity to experiment with new experiences while not having to be totally absorbed with security issues.

Shortly after arriving in this new job and in this new town, she became very anxious. Again in a very nonpredictable fashion she sought help from a therapist. When one considers her background, it is amazing that when she found herself in trouble, she had sufficient trust to reach out for help from another human being.

As an aside we should mention that we are not presenting this case because of some great therapeutic accomplishment. We do feel there were positive developments, but the main purpose in presenting this case is that it helps to separate traditional therapies from the service systems which we have been focusing on in this book. This is a client who was served in the community in a nontraditional fashion.

When she initially entered therapy, it was assumed that she would be treated within the context of the usual psychotherapeutic models. That is, she was introduced to free association, it was assumed that she would develop a transference relationship with the therapist, and that through reflection and interpretation she would begin to develop insight and eventually bring things together. As expected, in the opening phase of treatment she "told her story." That is, she presented her life story, expressed her resentments about her past, and expressed her desire to be "normal."

It was not difficult to diagnose almost immediately several major problems. Her basic patterns of identification were extremely confused and disturbed at all levels. She was unable to decide whether she was a man or a woman. Joan preferred homosexuality but had never managed to develop this kind of relationship. Her preference was for older women with large breasts who would in a consistent fashion care for her. The problems of identification went deeper than simply sexual choice—she really wanted someone to take over her life and take the responsibility for decision-making. There were times when Joan became immobilized and was unable to make decisions. She would become bogged down, until she was almost overwhelmed. She would then respond in an impulsive, irrational fashion, thus breaking through the bind of her indecisiveness.

Because of her identity issues, it was extremely difficult for her to develop a close or intimate relation. If she became intimate with another person, she would begin to lose her identity and become confused about the relationship. It would not be long before she would feel that the other person was attempting to take advantage of her or control her (paranoid feelings). However, instead of becoming paranoid, she would find a justification for running away from the relationship.

It was conjectured by the therapist that the homosexuality was a defense against her incestuous feelings toward her father and Joan's great fear of her mother's violent incestuous accusations and threats. She had definitely made a decision that she would not compete with women for men.

In traditional concepts the problems described are considered serious. There are residential facilities whose primary purpose is to serve persons with Joan's kind of deep identity issues. They feel that in working with this kind of problem the therapist has to be involved with the patient's entire life space. Even if it were desirable for Joan to be in this kind of facility, she would never have the money for this experience. These agencies are for the "super plus" person. Placing a person with deep identity issues in a state hospital can only be destructive.

For approximately six months the therapist continued to serve her within the traditional therapy model. There would be periods in which Joan seemed to be able to utilize this model for growth, but it would be only for brief spurts. After periods of apparent movement, she would "act out" in an impulsive fashion, undoing weeks of therapeutic effort. In the years during which the therapist knew the patient, she developed an elaborate repertoire of "acting out" patterns: experimenting with suicide, attempting to treat herself with tranquilizers which she obtained from her place of employment, making homosexual passes at nonhomosexual women, squandering her funds so that she was unable to pay for therapy, running up bills, quitting jobs without having other positions available, etc.

In traditional therapy, "acting out" is considered counterproductive and can be a reason for the therapist to terminate the relationship. The therapist in this situation knew that Joan needed help, and it did not seem appropriate to terminate her because she did not fit the model. It seemed more reasonable to alter the service system. This client was not able to grow through the utilization of the usual therapeutic technology.

It became clear that Joan through her first eighteen years of life did not have many of the experiences by which people grow. Many of the impulsive acting-out patterns were really her attempts to experiment and experience patterns of life that had not been available to her. Instead of dictating a style of life or attempting to interpret her behavior in psychological terminology, the therapist decided on a different approach. If the patient announced that she was going to "act out," the therapist asked her if she wanted to discuss it. If she did not want to discuss it, the matter would be dropped. If she decided to talk about the "acting out," the therapist would discuss the behavior and the possible consequence. At times the therapist, knowing he could not stop the behavior, would suggest procedures for reducing consequences; i.e., at times he would help her "beat the system."

Most "acting out" was reported after the fact, with the patient in an acute anxiety about the consequences. The situation would be discussed in detail, with the therapist functioning in a co-problem-solving role. The therapist would never warn her against future "acting out." This decision still remained with her. If the patient was fired from her job because of her behavior, the therapist did everything in his power to help her obtain another position. When the patient became acutely anxious, the therapist would utilize the therapeutic technology as a "first-aid measure." When the patient acted out against the therapist by not paying her bill, she found that he was prepared to take legal action against her.

On a number of occasions, the patient began to see the therapist as a manipulating and malevolent authority figure and she would then run away from therapy as she had run away from home. There were a number of such events, and when Joan was prepared to return to therapy, she was accepted back under the previous format. Some of these breaks lasted as long as a year. The basic themes of the therapy were to provide possible experiences for growth, to provide forms of help that might typically come from family members which were not available in her situation, and to utilize traditional therapeutic technology as a "first aid" device.

This is not a happy ending story. We will tell you "where she is" at this point in her life. She has completely separated herself from her parents. She has made a tentative commitment to homosexuality, having become active in the gay liberation movement. At this time she has a good skilled position and is at her high point in money-making. However, she decided that she does not like her position and is preparing to quit and run to another state. At the same time, she is taking a course in philosophy and is considering making a commitment to college and a possible career. Recently she had an argument with her therapist over a bad check she had given him, and she is threatening to quit therapy.

We have presented this case to demonstrate options to the usual therapy technology. The therapist, or problem solver, finding that the patient could not utilize traditional therapy procedures, attempted to find new ways of serving the client. This seems preferable to labeling the client as having a bad prognosis and extruding her from society. Problem-solving is at the heart of any meaningful service system.

In the final chapter we will attempt to bring together a developing game plan. This will include a number of innovations emerging from several creative caregivers. As we stated earlier, we will not present specific answers but rather introduce a viable process.

# VIII

## Pulling It Together

It is the feeling of the authors that the content of this last chapter can best be expressed from a personal perspective. We will, as we did in portions of Chapter V, move from the pronoun "we" to the pronoun "I." The senior author, Walter Fisher, will attempt to bring things together.

Although this is the final section of the book, it is certainly not the end of the story. In essence, this book portrays a longitudinal or historical perspective of my perceptions. I believe that my thinking is still in transit or in process, and I hope it will always be in transit. In this highly subjective field, it is a form of arrogance to believe that you have found a great "truth." Despite the lack of experimental support, it is amazing to discover how many famous names declare that their position is the "truth" and have assigned themselves the role of "apostle." No other branch of medicine would market a medical product on the flimsy support available for treatment models in mental health.

This easy acceptance of the validity of treatment systems is true not only of the famous names but is characteristic of most caregivers. For fifteen years I accepted the Medical-Freudian game plan as a "truth." Like a Talmudic or medieval scholar, I studied the works of Freud as if they were the Bible. I believed that there was no client who ever lived whom I would not be

able to classify into the flexible Freudian model. Armed with
the magical terminology, I categorized and treated clients in
my agency and in private practice. In addition, I was a zealous
missionary proselytizing among caregivers for a hundred miles
around. Those psychologists who could not see the "truths"
had a poor prognosis for future employment in the service
field. Most universities, though with a different orientation,
maintain the delusion of predicting who will be effective workers. They have been slow to catch on to the "joke."

Some of the hostility I expressed toward the Freudian model
is really anger directed toward myself. The anger does not
stem from the Medical-Freudian system being a false idol, but
rather because it is of such limited value. In terms of dollar
expenditures per day on mental health patients, there is very
little money to be spent. The Medical-Freudian model is extremely expensive, complicated, and lengthy. The model allows us to serve only a minimum number of clients. I find it an
incredible paradox that so many alleged "good Samaritan"
caregivers are willing to sit in their offices seeing one patient at
a time for many years and yet see themselves as meaningfully
serving the society in which they live. In fact, they see this
model to be the epitome of humanistic psychology. I have
become sufficiently cynical to believe that a good number of
caregivers who are categorized as professionals—i.e., received
their credentials through university certification—operate
through a service model which is primarily for their own
benefit.

In our agency, as in most mental health agencies, those persons classified as professionals only want to work with the
best-developed patients on Monday through Friday from 8:00
A.M. to 4:00 P.M. If a patient becomes violent, most professionals with their "super" techniques clear the "combat zone"
and "allow" the nonprofessionals the "opportunity" to pick up
the pieces. I recently heard a so-called professional person
say: "I make too much money to do this hard and dangerous

work. It is bad for the morale of the technicians who make less money to see me perform in the same task." I find this absurd and scandalous.

I have moved away from this Freudian dream to an approach that I can only describe with a number of adjectives: sociological, environmental, practical, pragmatic, historical, and social. In Chapters III and VII we provided case descriptions of a therapist altering his technology in order to provide more relevant services to patients who would traditionally have been described as poor prognostic risks. I would say that these are partial applications of what I am attempting to say. I will in this chapter, in as informal and personal a manner as possible, state my position. I would like to begin this process by describing a group module experience that I recently initiated.

## A GROUP AS A "MODULE OF EXPERIENCE"

It would be helpful to make several statements before I describe the actual group experience. At this point in my career I am an administrator in a state hospital. In this position I am not involved in what is usually called direct clinical service. When I was first employed at the hospital I functioned as a clinical psychologist, but I have since been promoted to an administrative position. In my current job my responsibilities are very much in the generalist category.

Even at this point in history, when I attempt to describe my work activities to academic acquaintances or most practicing clinical psychologists they prefer to classify or stereotype me as a nonclinician. From their perspective they seem to feel more comfortable if they can categorize persons in my role as business administrator types. For them, clinical services still represent the direct application of a particular technology to the patient. As I see my role it is that of a strategist or a tactician—someone who will help create and support the development of "modules of experience" that will provide hospital residents new opportunities to grow. The development of patient government groups, the introduction of a new profession, hospital reorganization, and the creation of new philosophies and ideologies are examples of administrative strategies. However, it is important that we do not become locked in these new administrative maneuvers. Many of the strategies are initially effective but later become serious problems.

The Department of Mental Health in Illinois in the early 1960's supported the concept of quick discharges in their doctrine of the "revolving door." This, in effect, means that recidivism is better than a continuous stay in the residential agencies. As part of this doctrine there developed in our state numerous nursing homes and sheltered-care facilities operated by private owners. This policy played a major role in drastically reducing the population of patients in state hospitals. In this sense it was a very effective policy. However, recently there has been an enormous community eruption against the placement of large numbers of former patients in concentrated community areas. These concentrations are now labeled as "mental health ghettos." This is, of course, resulting in a revision and restricting of department policy.

During the last decade, almost the entire effort of our agency has been focused on administrative strategies. In fact, most of the clever and creative clinicians have moved into the administrative roles. During this period there has been an emphasis in our agency on the theme "treatment through administrative change." Unfortunately, this focus has resulted in less energy and creativity being funneled into direct clinical service and mental health technology.

With the creative people moving into administrative positions, the remaining clinicians have tended to remain in traditional treatment modules. They insist that these are the "quality" treatment procedures. The fact that they cannot define "quality," or that they are utterly unable to evaluate their services, does not in any way prevent them from rationalizing their lack of production behind this semantically meaningless term. We find many employees attempting to utilize therapeutic variations of psychoanalysis. There are prolonged clinical staff meetings that tie up a large proportion of the caregivers in redundant patterns of activity. There are entire programs involved in endless administrative staff meetings in which spineless and dependent employees sit about crying on one another's shoulders and hoping that someone else will make their decision for them.

Although these conditions have long angered me, I had little opportunity to experiment with the clinical technology. However, a short time ago a psychology intern asked if I would be willing to provide some training for several of the young psychologists. In the course of the conversation, it occurred to me that this might be an opportunity to experiment with a group approach which would reflect the theoretical orientation that has been developing in this book. As far as I am concerned, learning in the clinical field can best take place through the apprentice model rather than in a university setting. We decided that the interns and I would work with a group of patients in something akin to a group-therapy system.

SELECTION OF THE GROUP

We determined that our group of patients should come from the Extended Care Service. These are patients who did not respond to care in the Acute Service (ninety days or less). Our Acute Service inpatient programs still function primarily in the Medical-Freudian model and their therapeutic technology is essentially that which the public equates with treatment.

The Extended Care Service has not been utilizing group therapy because most of its patients have not been able to utilize this "module of experience" for growth. I felt that this might be a chance to innovate a group technology for highly regressed persons: the noncommunicative, incontinent, poorly clothed, withdrawn, and apathetic. I had an Extended Care Service team leader select patients who fitted this highly regressed pattern.

I should state that we, the psychology interns and myself, decided to conduct this group activity in our Audio-Visual Service. The primary reason for putting it on film was to utilize it for training. In addition I think that it is important to make clinical activities as public as possible in order to eliminate mysticism and mythology from the process. I think that much of the stupidity in the field of mental health has been perpetrated by the privacy and secretiveness which marks the entire operation. (I also would not want to rule out my potential ham quality.)

BASIC THERAPEUTIC CONTRACT

I tend to start new group sessions with the minimum of preconceptions and demands. Initially, I left attendance at the meetings on a voluntary basis. If the patient did not want to attend, that was the individual's decision, but if he or she chose to attend, he or she had to remain until the session was over. We later modified this decision, but I will discuss this when I report on the group process. It was decided that the group would have ten one-hour sessions, and at that point the group would be dissolved. This latter decision was made for several reasons: limitations on my time, a desire to study the impact of the time limitation on the patients' behavior, resource limitations of our Audio-Visual Service, and because in some ways I feel boundaries are important.

It was also part of the group contract that as a small society they would have the right to examine the contract, and within limitations, alter it when necessary. It was set up as an open group in that new members might join us anytime during the ten sessions.

## FIRST SESSION

I will not differentiate the various meetings except for this initial session. It was during this first meeting that we began to establish the routine and set the stage for future events. In the first several minutes the group leaders established the ritual of each of us identifying ourselves and made it clear that we would continue this introducing process until we were sure that we were all acquainted with one another. It was my plan that the remainder of the meeting would have minimal structure except for the basic contract described in the previous section, unless someone became violent. For most of the hour, we had a scene reminiscent of a "snake pit." One of the men rolled himself up into a fetal posture. A middle-aged woman talked incessantly and suddenly ran from the room. Another woman had a continuous change of facial expressions that were not congruent with happenings at the session. There was a young man who appeared to be under such incredible tension that he seemingly found it impossible to sit. He performed rituals, exercised, walked around the room, and attempted literally to shake off the tension. There was no communication among the patients. Each of them "did their thing" oblivious of everything or everyone else. I would say that we came closest to communication, or relating, around their common need for cigarettes or lights and my ability to provide cigarettes.

These were all long-term patients who for years had been served by the Medical-Freudian model in the sense that they were described as schizophrenic and as having a poor prognosis. If I were to attempt to treat them by finding the cause of their "disease" and attempting to "cure" them, I would expect that I would need institutionalization myself. In actuality my approach is practical, parsimonious, and as simple as possible.

At the end of the first meeting, I decided upon a method. An effort would be made to meet some of their needs; e.g., the staff would begin to provide cigarettes at each session, and with each new meeting we would add new "goodies" such as coffee, cookies, ice cream. In addition, at the beginning of each meeting we would take requests in regard to current needs; e.g., help them retrieve missing clothing, aid them in obtaining false teeth, or expedite their receiving privileges. It seems to me that all human services must begin with the identification and/or understanding of basic needs and motivations. We were to use the "goodies" as a reward-deprivation model to influence their behavior.

The second major thrust was to be staff's refusal to accept or tolerate the patients' "crazy" behavior. The patients had to understand the conditions for acceptability; i.e., responsible behavior would be rewarded and deviant behavior would not be tolerated. Therapeutic contracts between staff and patients would be binding on staff only if the patients functioned in a responsible fashion. We would in no way do business with the bizarre, grotesque, infantile, side of the client.

## SUBSEQUENT SESSIONS

In subsequent sessions we have maintained our procedure of each person introducing himself. We have not yet reached the point where all of them know each other. In the second meeting we announced our new format, which included the reward system and the limit-setting. Patients still had the right not to attend therapy, but this became a privilege for those individuals who did not behave "crazily." The interactions will be better understood if we describe the behavior of specific patients. One of our female patients refused to cooperate in any way. Her main form of "crazy" behavior was to maintain a constant flow of words with no apparent connections. Someone aptly labeled her "the Dictionary." Her incessant outpouring of words interfered with an already malfunctioning communication network. The group, with some pressure from myself, agreed that we should have a courtesy rule that persons should talk in turn with only one person holding the floor at a time. She, of course, refused to live by the rules. We initiated a process of escalation, starting with polite requests and withdrawing of goodies until we finally moved her bodily away from the group and placed her in the corner. She did become quiet once we put her in the corner, but after a lapse of five minutes she urinated over herself and the floor. We then forced her to clean the floor with paper toweling rather than with a mop.

Another patient rested in his chair in a fetal position. When we talked to him he spoke in a barely audible and nonconnected language system. We requested that he sit properly, talk clearly and loudly, and that he respond in a relevant fashion. He did not choose to resist our demands. We were obviously offering him "a contract that he could not turn down."

One more example of a problem and an approach. This will be done dialogue style paraphrased in terms of a discussion in the second session.

GROUP LEADER: Why are you here, Robert?

PATIENT: I guess that I am a sex maniac. (His appearance is that of a Caspar Milquetoast.)

GROUP LEADER (*laughs*): What do you mean you're a sex maniac?

PATIENT: I keep "jacking off." I can't help it.

GROUP LEADER: How long have you been in the hospital with this problem?

PATIENT: Twenty-five years.

GROUP LEADER: Why in the hell don't you stop it? You must like being in a hospital.

PATIENT: I can't help it. I am mentally ill.

GROUP LEADER: There is no such thing as mental illness. You are afraid to live out in the world—it is strictly a "cop-out." You want somebody to take care of you.

PATIENT: I am sick and you'll have to take care of me. I'll get a lawyer—I'll get Raymond Burr!

GROUP LEADER (*a lot of laughing*): I'll get Owen Marshall! (At this point everyone in the group is laughing and different members of the group are saying they will get Judd or Perry Mason.)

We are refusing to accept the patient's "craziness" and are prepared to use our "power" to interrupt patienthood. In many ways all service models have a strong control and power component. We should say that this is similar to the methodology utilized with the earlier reported individual cases. This, like all models, will result in changes in behavior, but it will not result in a "cure"; nor is it intended to.

### CONCLUSIONS ON GROUP EXPERIENCE

In this group experience I am not attempting to establish causes for deviance or give insight, nor am I attempting to change the inner man. The focus is on behavioral changes and the staff expectancy—"you cannot be 'crazy.'" The patient's "craziness" is an expression of his defiance and resistance; i.e., deviance is the power system of the alienated people. They probably have a right to it, if one is willing to accept them in an institutionalized role. I decided that I would not accept this role, at least for the members of this group. We were applying pressure to force them to utilize socially accepted behavioral patterns. There is no question that they will capitulate and reorder their behavior. This kind of technology can be utilized by less-trained persons, with fewer staff, more patients, and with fewer dollars.

There will be those who will holler that this is not "quality treatment" or that I am being inhuman. So far as I am concerned, neither accusation is true. Traditional therapists will not work with these patients. If they did work with them, it would be a ten-year project. The true sadism is to ignore these patients and to allow them to deteriorate on a back ward.

The problem is, of course, to establish a technology that will provide these patients with a "module of experience" which will allow them to grow. I do not feel that the technique we described above is the only available approach to serve this type of client. In recent years many facilities have developed a new service module that has been labeled as "behavior modification" or "behavioral analysis." In essence this is a procedure in which a patient is literally paid for behavior the therapist wishes to support (reinforce), or punished for behavior the therapist wishes to eliminate. As I said earlier, I believe that if you had enough money you could literally buy away a major portion of "crazy" behavior. We recently examined our budget to assess funds available for this program and found that it comes to seven cents per day for each patient. It is the same old story—"losers" under stress have few options other than becoming "crazy." When we attempt to buy their symptoms, we have a total resource of seven cents per day. It is impossible to consider service without considering cost and available resources.

## BASIC BELIEFS

I am concluding this book in terms of what I think the reader will want. At this point, I feel certain that many readers will be saying, "He has assaulted most of the existing systems, but he has not provided us with clear alternatives." It is probably fair to provide guidelines, beliefs, assumptions, and philosophies. I will attempt to tell you where I am, but it is important to remember that I am in transit. It is my hope that by the time the reader has this book available, I will have moved beyond these beliefs. The themes to be presented are not meant to be swallowed; it is my intention that this material will trigger a process which will carry each person through his own trajectory with his own unique solutions.

## I. A HUMAN SERVICES "INDUSTRY"

I like to think that the services which I make available fall in the category of a human services "industry." Within such an "industry" the caregiver has the task of aiding the person to become productive. By productive, I mean that the individual is pursuing his goals in a culturally acceptable fashion and that the goals and means are under his *volitional control*. It might be helpful in understanding this approach to use a brief case presentation.

### Case Presentation

A man in his middle twenties came for psychotherapeutic help because he was depressed, bored, easily fatigued, and disgusted with life. I should say that there were many problems with his wife and girl friend, and clinical probing brought to the surface "juicy" early dynamics. Along with the broad clinical picture of distress it became clear that he was extremely dissatisfied with his work situation. He was in a dead-end job, had no career series, and each day of work was unpleasant, unsatisfactory, and meaningless. Instead of attempting to work with the inner man, I decided that I would help him by seeing if I could aid him in regard to his career plans. In his position he worked as a business person, in mainly accounting-like tasks, in a factory that placed a premium on a college degree. Although he was an intelligent man, he had quit high school in disgust, married early, and had not pursued any formal studies since the age of seventeen. I told him about the possibilities of examinations for school credit, and in quick succession, with minimal preparation, he obtained a high school degree and an Associate of Arts degree. His company paid for course work, and in two years on a part-time basis he completed his third year of college. At this point his wife went to work, he quit his job, and he obtained several loans that allowed him to attend college on a full-time basis. Within three years he received a Master of Arts degree in social work. This is the type of employment that he had always wanted. During these years I saw the patient on occasion for "first aid." This story, of course, does not have a true happy ending. He is certainly not now a "normal" man. As it turned out, he not only changed jobs but shed his first and second wives. He is currently on his third wife, and this is probably a more adaptive situation. This person started a process that is still going on. In some ways he is more actively pursuing his goals and his dreams, and I honestly believe he is more productive.

## II. IDENTIFYING THE DOMINANT NEED SYSTEM

At the heart of any of the caregiving models is the tapping and understanding of need systems, motivations, and basic human attachments. Regardless of approach, if we are to serve our consumer in a meaningful fashion, we have to identify the dominant need system. Psychoanalysts utilize free association as their means for identifying the basic wish of the client. They assume that the primary motivational system organizes and directs the behavior of the individual. To change the individual we have to alter the dominant motive. In the patient government group that we discussed in Chapter III, we had the patients express their needs in terms of formalized proposals. In this type of model one accepts the client's own identification of need at face value. Most organizations utilize a variety of procedures to tap employee needs and frustrations resulting from unmet needs: suggestion boxes, utilization of the ombudsman, joint management and union meetings, and a variety of communication networks. In the discussion of the group experience with the deeply regressed patients mentioned earlier in this chapter, we were primarily oriented toward identifying the need systems and working with these patients in the context of their needs.

I think that of all the writers in the mental health field, Hansell (1970) has done the best job of organizing an operationally definable motivational system. Hansell is, without question, one of the more creative and innovative caregivers on the current scene. I would like to present schematically his system.

Hansell assumes that adults residing in our culture require certain attachments in order to maintain their equilibrium. If the individual fails to make any one of these attachments, he develops a stress reaction that results in an emotional crisis. I should say that these attachments are basic needs of the organism.

## Hansell's Seven Essential Attachments

1. The organism has a need to take in food, oxygen, and information. The monitoring of food deprivation and oxygen deprivation is obvious. When there is an insufficiency of information this is expressed by loss of curiosity, boredom, and feelings of not being stimulated.

2. A continuing intimate relationship with another person. This is not simply sexual intimacy but a deep personal experience. This can be monitored by reports or lack of reports on intimacy.

3. There is a need for each individual to be part of a social network. This typically means that the person belongs to a social group, a church group, or a club. This is monitored by the individual's feeling that he is a member of a network and that he feels a solidarity with this group and they with him.

4. There is a need for a person to have a defined identity. This can be monitored by the individual's clarity in regard to his own identity: "I know who I am. This behavior is consistent with my identity." It is also an identity

that he cherishes. It isn't particularly important whether or not the therapist likes it.

5. The individual has a social role that provides him with a sense of competence or excellence. It is an attachment to one persisting role for which there are established lines of excellence and there is dignity conferred for the excellence. The attachment can be monitored by the presence of self-esteem (a feeling of well-being).

6. There is a need by the individual to be tied into the cash economy either through his own work efforts or a relationship with a person who has earning power. This can be monitored by the presence of purchasing power on a continuing basis.

7. Each person must have a comprehensive system of meaning. It allows us to develop priorities that aid us in making difficult choices between options. This is monitored by the individual's ability to make decisions.

## Failure to Make Attachments: Crises

As stated above, if any of the seven attachments are not made, the individual suffers a crisis. Hansell believes that all individuals in crisis have common characteristics.

1. The person is unable to maintain a fixed attention. There is rapid switching of focused attention from object to object.

2. Although there is a flight of attention, there is a preoccupation with certain fixed topics, e.g., sin, death, and destruction.

3. Affectional ties to the various attachments are loosened. There is less interaction and less intimacy with one's social network. At the same time, there is an increased capacity for making new attachments.

4. The individual's identity becomes more diffuse as he is less clear as to what he values in himself. At the same time, he develops an increased capacity for entering into new identities.

5. The social role performance of the individual deterio-rates. However, he has heightened ability to practice new roles.
6. There is a reduced ability to make decisions.
7. The person has increased recall ability but on a random basis.

### Assessing Broken Attachments

Hansell's service model is organized around the seven at-tachments and the crises that result when one or more attach-ments are violated. Basically Hansell is a problem solver, so that when a patient arrives at his front door in crisis and seek-ing help, a problem-solving process is initiated. It begins with an assessment process in which large amounts of information are systematically gathered. The problem solver in this system gathers information about the seven attachments, attempting to discover which attachment or attachments have been broken. In essence this is a diagnostic system. This is done as part of a screening-linking-planning conference. Hansell sug-gests the following arrangements for these conferences:

1. Physical Setting
   a. Room with seating capacity for ten to fifteen persons
   b. Conference phone arrangement
   c. All available resources
2. Agencies: multiagency participation
3. The individual's social network should be available
4. Objectives of the conference
   a. Allow the individual to demonstrate cherished behav-ior
   b. The network should notice and reinforce the cherished behavior
   c. Attempt to stimulate the client's coping or adaptive mechanisms
   d. The agency people should prepare service techniques to cope with the potential troubles that might develop

It is hoped that through these conferences the client will be able to reestablish his lost attachments and that this will resolve the crisis. In essence this is a crisis intervention model that Hansell has designed to provide "front line" service and prevent the consumer from becoming institutionalized.

There will be some who will question the validity of Hansell's concepts as well as his service module. I would think that Hansell would be the first to say that his system is in process and that he does not see it as an ultimate "truth." However, it is a relatively new option for consumers and is frequently an alternative to institutionalization in a state hospital. In this sense it is what we describe as an alternative "module of experience" and an example of "treatment through institutional change."

### III. NEW "MODULES OF EXPERIENCE"

When I talked earlier about the need for new "modules of experience" I was referring to such efforts as those of Hansell. It is the lack of this type of creativity, and the sticking to the same "old guns," that has left us in our current dilemma. There are endless numbers of human needs that we do not know how to meet or that we do not meet because of societal restrictions. We have had patients living in our agency for decades under the restriction that they should not engage in sexuality. This is not a burden we would want to place on the strongest person. We not only place this restriction in regard to ward behavior, but somehow staff members seem to become upset and angry when they encounter sexual behavior anywhere on the agency grounds. Recently a man who describes himself as a "professional person" complained because a patient had been masturbating in front of his office for six and a half months. I am not sure why this totally resourceless person took six months to react to this "poor soul."

Another employee confronted with a similar situation returned the patient to the ward and explained that the patient was exposing himself in a public place. The first man chose to write a memo that was carried to the superintendent and that described the terrible upset he experienced watching this man masturbate for half a year.

At about the same time that the superintendent received the memo from the anguished professional, the following report was received from our security police: "At 12:45 P.M. on Tuesday, May 2, 1972, Security Officers John Doe and John Jones responded to a radio call to proceed immediately to Building I, where a male and a female patient were engaged in an oral sex act in the washroom."

There were only female employees on duty at the time and they were reluctant to interfere with the couple, identified as ———— and ————, both Building I residents. Officers Doe and Jones proceeded to Building I, where, as ordered (as an aside there is no one there who has the authority to *order* them), they assisted in restraining patient ————. Two of my staff had decided that oral sexuality was a police matter. The clever security police in their report (the local gossip column) were, in effect, saying, Guess what nice young couple was engaging in oral sexuality?

When one becomes aware of a mental institution staff's inability to cope with sex, it is interesting to consider what message is communicated to the residents. The absolute absurdity of the situation becomes clear when you realize that prisons and mental hospitals have had their sexual problems from their inception and only now, a million years later, a few prisons are beginning to make arrangements for married prisoners and their spouses to have intercourse. This latter solution is, of course, an attempt to make a new "module of experience" available to its inmates.

Every community has mores, taboos, laws, rules, and values that interfere with the growth of the individual. The paradox we have in regard to sexual problems exists in a variety of forms in every village, town, and city in the country. There is a small town near our agency in which a significant number of persons in the community oppose sexual education in the school. There are endless paradoxes like this in every cultural unit.

Let us consider Hansell's seven attachments. Suppose we accept his attachments as representative of human needs. If we *assume* that making these seven attachments is essential for making an adequate adaptation, then I would conclude that caregivers must involve themselves in those roles which will help the patient to meet his needs. That is, the caregivers must be clever problem solvers and expediters. I would like to provide several more examples of attempts at problem-solving.

Mowrer (1966a) has been concerned with the human need to be part of a social group. Mowrer says: "[There are] many other sources of evidence that the Small Group is indeed emerging as a new *primary social institution* [italics mine]. How it will be related to the more traditional primary groups is still an open question, but there is at least some basis for speculation in this connection. Small groups may help stabilize the nuclear family by providing a kind of substitute for the extended family which has become almost nonexistent in our society for great masses of people." Mowrer goes on to develop the theme that such small groups "may largely replace the Established Church." He has developed a new group institution which he calls an "integrity group." For details on the operation of this system the reader will have to go to the original source. The crucial point for this book is Mowrer's development of a new type of peer group that will serve as a meaningful "module of experience" at literally no expense for large numbers of persons who are cut off from a social network.

Another meaningful social institution has been the development of the "career series." There are numerous persons in this society who have become alienated and nonproductive because they are locked into their jobs. A "career series" that allows a person to move ahead in his occupation on the basis of his personal competence provides a marvelous incentive to mold the alienated person into a productive individual. This can be extremely important in developing a social role.

There have been many attempts to find new ways to link the disadvantaged person into a cash economy. Unfortunately caregivers have not identified with the problems and the proposed solutions. However, the eventual emergence of a guaranteed annual income will play an important role in reducing maladaptive behavior. With enough available cash, we can probably wipe out those maladaptations which we have seen as being characteristic of the lower socioeconomic groups.

There have been numerous clever innovations in problem-solving. A number of these we have discussed: Szasz's ideology, Glass's combat psychiatry themes, the creation of new professions, the "revolving door" philosophy, the geographical, or catchment, programs, "treatment through institutional change," the development of the human service model, etc.

It is extremely important to be open-minded and not be trapped by old prejudices. The other day the father of one of our patients came to my office. He was upset and distressed because of the attitude of the hospital staff. His daughter had been in and out of Elgin State Hospital since the early 1950's. At this point several staff members were announcing that she was never going to get better, and why help her find another position, since she lost her last one after seven months. Prior to that, she had lost her job after two years. The staff working directly with her was discouraged, but I would prefer to see this in-and-out pattern as a style of life rather than her remaining in the institution on a continuous basis. It seems reasonable that some people require occasional sanctuary.

In fact, during the next several decades, before public health and prevention models become effective, it does not seem out of the question that we will establish brief temporary sanctuaries for some of our repeating customers, e.g., alcoholics, drug addicts, and inadequate personalities. I am not saying this is true, but it is an option to consider.

The heart of the task is to arrive at new creative solutions for meeting the needs of our consumers. There are many possible solutions to problems, but our theoretical "blinders" have kept us locked into a few alternatives. In concluding this section I want to quote from a newspaper column by Sydney J. Harris in the May 8, 1972, *Chicago Daily News*. Although acupuncture is the key theme of the article, it is not my primary focus. I mainly want to present an early health insurance system mentioned in the article.

In ancient China the patient paid the doctor while he was well and stopped paying only when he fell ill. It was the task of the doctor whom he visited every three to six months to keep him well, and for this he paid a fixed fee. When he took ill, he suspended payments until he was cured or much improved. Consider the built-in motivation for the physician to serve his client.

## IV. CONTINUING REASSESSMENT OF CAREGIVING SERVICES

I believe that all caregiving services should be assessed in terms of overall cost and detailed expenditures for various services: e.g., How much money was spent on group therapy or individual therapy? Many communities have as their primary mental health service a traditional clinic. Attentive publics and consumers do not have sufficient information to monitor the operation of these facilities. These clinics have to be evaluated not only in terms of clients seen but also in terms of clients they have failed to see. There are still clinics that maintain long waiting lists. This can only be viewed as a scandalous absurdity. These clinics as solutions to community maladaptation problems have been obsolete for ten years and still, because of lack of information, they continue to exist. Informa-

tion is the most meaningful technique to eliminate obsolete
institutions.

## V. BASING SERVICES ON A SOCIOLOGICAL MODEL

I do think caregivers should become extremely active in
community affairs both in their caregiver roles and as citizens.
It seems to me to be an inescapable conclusion that the massive impact of political systems, economic practices, and social
systems makes most service modules insignificant. A number
of the staff members at our agency have formed their own community group, called GROW (this is not an acronym), in
which their goal is to influence community attitudes and ulti-
mately to influence legislators. I do feel that the great forces in
molding persons are environmental and sociological. It is our
*assumption* that services should for the greater part be cast
into a sociological model rather than into an intraorganismic
approach.

## VI. ALTERING BEHAVIOR, NOT THE INNER MAN

Because of our ultimate ignorance I think that services
should be as simple and as parsimonious as possible. The goal
of the caregiver should be to alter the behavior of the client
and not the inner man.

## VII. PUBLIC HEALTH, OR PREVENTION, SYSTEMS

It seems to me that the ultimate service model should be a
public health, or prevention, system. We have to understand
the "modules of experiences" that allow the individual to grow
and make these experiences available to everyone. I would
personally like to invest my energy in this direction.

There are many other things to be said, but I feel that we
have provided our reader with sufficient input at this time. I

am sure that some persons will become angry because they will feel that we are being destructive toward existing systems. I would prefer to think that we are providing new perspectives and additional options. We would hope that we are triggering a process, or functioning as catalysts in "turning people on," or turning them in new directions in regard to the key issues in the human service area.

# References

Adler, Alfred, *The Practice and Theory of Individual Psychology.* Harcourt, Brace and Company, Inc., 1924.

Barton, Russell, *Institutional Neurosis.* Bristol, England: John Wright & Sons Ltd., 1959 (American ed., The Williams & Wilkins Company, 1966).

Bleuler, Eugen, *Dementia praecox oder Gruppe der Schizophrenien.* Leipzig and Vienna: Franz Deuticke, 1911. (American ed., *Dementia Praecox or the Group of Schizophrenias,* tr. by Joseph Zinkin. International Universities Press, 1966.)

Bower, Philip, *Rorschach Diagnosis by Systematic Combining of Content, Thought Process, and Determinant Scales,* Genetic Psychology Monograph, Vol. 62 (1960), pp. 105–183.

Caplan, Gerald, *Principles of Preventive Psychiatry.* Basic Books, Inc., Publishers, 1964.

Cumming, John, and Cumming, Elaine, *Ego and Milieu: The Theory and Practice of Environmental Therapy.* Atherton Press, 1962.

Dewey, John, *Education Today,* ed. by Joseph Ratner. Greenwood Press, 1940.

Erikson, Erik H., *Childhood and Society.* W. W. Norton & Company, Inc., 1950.

Erikson, Erik H., *Young Man Luther*. W. W. Norton & Company, Inc., 1958.

Fisher, Walter, "The Elgin Model: A Traits-Values-Dynamics Psychodiagnostic System." Paper presented at the meeting of the American Psychological Association, Los Angeles, September, 1965a.

Fisher, Walter, "Social Change as a Therapeutic Tool in a Closed Institution," *Psychotherapy*, Vol. 2, No. 3 (October, 1965b).

Fisher, Walter, Mehr, Joseph, and Truckenbrod, Philip, "Critical Mass No. 1: Treatment Through Institutional Change." Unpublished manuscript, Elgin State Hospital, Elgin, Illinois, 1971a.

Fisher, Walter, Mehr, Joseph, and Truckenbrod, Philip, "Critical Mass No. 2: Assumptions, Implications, and Problem-solving in Treatment Through Institutional Change." Unpublished manuscript, Elgin State Hospital, Elgin, Illinois, 1971b.

Freud, Sigmund, *A General Introduction to Psychoanalysis*. Boni & Liveright, 1920.

Freud, Sigmund, "The Psychopathology of Everyday Life," in A. A. Brill (ed.), *The Basic Writings of Sigmund Freud*. Random House, Inc., 1938.

Freud, Sigmund (1938), *An Outline of Psychoanalysis*. W. W. Norton & Company, Inc., 1949.

Freud, Sigmund (1937), "Analysis Terminable and Interminable," in *Collected Papers*, Vol. 5, tr. by Joan Riviere. London: Hogarth Press, 1950.

Freud, Sigmund, *The Complete Works of Sigmund Freud*. The Macmillan Company, 1964.

Glass, Albert J., "Psychotherapy in the Combat Zone." Symposium on Stress, Walter Reed Army Medical Center, Washington, D.C., 1953.

Glass, Albert J., "Principles of Combat Psychiatry," *Military Medicine*, Vol. 117, July, 1955.

Glover, Edward, *Technique of Psychoanalysis,* rev. ed. International Universities Press, 1968.

Goffman, Erving, *Asylums.* Doubleday & Company, Anchor Book, 1961.

Hanfmann, Eugenia, and Kasanin, J. S., *Conceptual Thinking in Schizophrenia.* Nervous and Mental Disease Monographs (No. 67), 1942.

Hansell, Norris, "Patient Predicament and Clinical Service," *Archives of General Psychiatry,* Vol. 17, August, 1967.

Hansell, Norris, "Casualty Management Method: An Aspect of Mental Health Technology in Transition," *Archives of General Psychiatry,* Vol. 19, September, 1968.

Hansell, Norris, "Introduction to the Screening-Linking-Planning Conference Method" ("Excerpts from Discussions of Triage Problems"). Unpublished manuscript, Northwestern Medical School, Chicago, Illinois. April, 1970.

Hollingshead, A. B., and Redlich, F. C., "Social Stratification and Psychiatric Disorders," in Ohmer Milton and Robert G. Wahler (eds.), *Behavior Disorders: Perspectives and Trends,* 2d ed. J. B. Lippincott Company, 1969.

Jones, M., McGee, R., and Grant, J., *Social Psychiatry.* London: Tavistock Publications Ltd., 1952.

Klein, Melanie, *Psychoanalysis of Children.* W. W. Norton & Company, Inc., 1932.

LeGuillant, L., "Une expérience de réadaptation sociale instituée par les événements de guerre," *Hyg. Men.,* Vol. 36 (1946–1947), pp. 85–102.

Martin, D. V., "Institutionalisation," *Lancet,* Vol. 2, December 3, 1955, pp. 1188–1190.

Menninger, Karl, "The Course of Illness," *Menninger Clinic Bulletin,* Vol. 25, No. 5 (September, 1961).

Moore, Wilbert E., *Social Change.* Prentice-Hall, Inc., 1963.

Mowrer, O. Hobart, "Guilt in the Social Sciences, or the Conflicting Doctrines of Determinism and Personal Accountability," in Helmut Schoeck and J. W. Wiggins (eds.), *Psy-*

*chiatry and Responsibility.* D. Van Nostrand Company, Inc., 1962.

Mowrer, O. Hobart, "Integrity Therapy: A Self-help Approach," *Psychotherapy,* Vol. 3, No. 3 (August, 1966a).

Mowrer, O. Hobart, "The Basis of Psychopathology: Malconditioning or Misbehavior?" *Journal of the National Association of Women Deans and Counselors.* Vol. XXIX, No. 2 (Winter, 1966b).

Piaget, Jean, *The Language and Thought of the Child,* 2d ed. London: George Routledge & Sons, Ltd., 1932 (American ed., Humanities Press, Inc., 1959).

Reich, W., *Charakteranalyse.* Vienna: Selbstverlag des Verfassers, 1933. (American ed., *Character Analysis.* Farrar, Straus & Young, Inc., 1949.)

Reik, Theodor, *Ritual: Psycho-analytic Studies,* tr. by Douglas Bryan (*Psychological Problems of Religion, No. 1*). Farrar, Straus & Company, Inc., 1946.

Reik, Theodor, *Listening with the Third Ear.* Pyramid Publications, Inc., 1964.

Rogers, Carl R., *Client-centered Therapy.* Houghton Mifflin Company, 1951.

Rowitz, Louis, and Levy, Leo, "The State Mental Hospital in Transition: An Approach to the Study of Mental Hospital Decentralization," *Mental Hygiene,* Vol. 55, No. 1 (January, 1971).

Russell, Bertrand, *A History of Western Philosophy.* Simon & Schuster, Inc., 1960.

Shakow, David, *The Nature of Deterioration in Schizophrenic Conditions.* Nervous and Mental Disease Monographs (No. 70), 1946.

Stekel, Wilhelm, *Conditions of Nervous Anxiety and Their Treatment,* tr. by Rosalie Gabler. Liveright Publishing Corporation, 1950.

Sullivan, Harry Stack, *The Interpersonal Theory of Psychiatry.* W. W. Norton & Company, 1953.

Szasz, Thomas S., *The Myth of Mental Illness.* A Hoeber-Harper book, Harper & Row, Publishers, Inc., 1961.

Szasz, Thomas S., "From the Slaughterhouse to the Mad House," *Psychotherapy,* Vol. 8, No. 1 (Spring, 1971).

Whyte, William H., *The Organization Man.* Simon & Schuster, Inc., 1956.

Wing, John K., "Institutionalism in Mental Hospitals," *British Journal of Social and Clinical Psychology,* Vol. 1 (1962), pp. 38–51.